THE MUSTARD COOKBOOK

BY SALLY AND MARTIN STONE

 AVON
PUBLISHERS OF BARD, CAMELOT AND DISCUS BOOKS

To Abby and Matt
with love

AVON BOOKS
A division of
The Hearst Corporation
959 Eighth Avenue
New York, New York 10019

Copyright © 1981 by Sally and Martin Stone
Book design by Joyce Kubat
Published by arrangement with the authors
Library of Congress Catalog Card Number: 80-69605
ISBN: 0-380-76844-5

First Avon Printing, April, 1981

AVON TRADEMARK REG. U.S. PAT. OFF.
AND IN OTHER COUNTRIES, MARCA
REGISTRADA, HECHO EN U.S.A.

Printed in the U.S.A.

ACKNOWLEDGMENTS

We would like to offer thanks to everyone who helped and encouraged us, particularly to our children, Abby and Matt, who lent us their tastebuds unflinchingly; to our friends Cynthia and Elliott and Dale and Liz and John and Jerry and Jack who put up with our singlemindedness during the difficult testing, tasting and retesting period; to our nieces and nephews who never complained even when their lips and tongues were singed; to Vicky for her errorless and tireless typing; to the Schlesinger Library for allowing us to sit on their floor and thumb through their enormously helpful collection of ancient and current food books; to our mothers, Flo, for contributing her marinated pepper recipe and recalling that she begged for mustard sandwiches when she was a child, and Sarah for her potato salad and early childhood inspiration; to Nancy for listening; to Ruth who's constant questions forced us to be clear and concise; to Renee Sonner who set aside her busy schedule to translate Dumas; to Barbara for finding Arnold and Elise; to Arnold and Elise for their advice and reassurance; and finally to Page Cuddy, our editor, who enthusiastically helped us to realize our goal and for her discreet and good humored criticism. We salute each other as well for weaving together the frayed nerves caused by collaborating on something other than marriage and children.

CONTENTS

INTRODUCTION

Mustard is one of the most neglected ingredients in the kitchen. So handy is the mustard jar on the table and so familiar are mustard's obvious uses, that many cooks often overlook its subtler applications.

It exists in four forms—whole seeds, dry powder, oil, and prepared paste—and can be used to season all kinds of things—salad dressings, rarebits, deviled dishes, in pickling, marinades, sauces, and creamed dishes. It enhances many ordinary dishes—sauerkraut, coleslaw, potato salad, poached fish, vegetables. It transforms others—soups, quiches, eggs, breads, crepes, soufflés, dumplings. It enlivens roasts, terrines, meat loafs, pâtés, stuffings, gravies, fruits—even cakes and cookies.

A cookbook devoted to mustard can only serve as a guide, a platform for innovation and experimentation. This is a sampling, a suggestion of how to use mustard in cooking. Your palate will be the best guide to other liaisons.

If you're unfamiliar with the different flavors of mustards available, it takes some experience to understand which ones to use with what. Some are salty, some are sweet, some are hot, sour, or bitter. You'll soon learn which mustards marry well with which foods.

And don't be surprised if, in several of the recipes, the spice seems to be anonymous. It isn't. The same dish would be very different without its addition. On the other hand, a recipe using only a small amount of mustard—a teaspoonful, perhaps—can be quite aromatic and have a piquancy that's completely unexpected. That's the interesting thing about mustard.

Though mustard appears in every recipe in this book, it should not find its way into every dish in a meal, no matter how much you like it. Orchestrate a menu for color, texture, nutrition, surprise—and for flavor contrasts and complements.

To guide you as you explore mustard cookery, each section includes tips for the clever use of mustard in your kitchen. These little hints will show you quick and easy ways to liven up your favorite recipes and get you accustomed to "thinking mustard" when you cook.

A whole new world of taste will open up to you when you begin using mustard as a seasoning.

MUSTARD: ITS HISTORY AND A CELEBRATION OF ITS USES

BEYOND THE HOT DOG

Mustard is the world's most popular seasoning; over 700 million pounds are consumed worldwide each year. More than 30 million gallons are used in the United States, yet only a small portion of that vast quantity is used as a cooking ingredient.

As a condiment it is unquestionably the star of the American dining table. What would a hot dog be without a tangy golden stripe painted down its middle? A soft pretzel isn't a soft pretzel in Pennsylvania without it. A naked pastrami on rye?

Ball-park mustard and delicatessen mustard, those are the two kinds we use from sea to shining sea—sunny yellow, dull brown, and shades in between. It is a cliché of luncheonette counters, hamburger havens, kosher delis, frankfurter stands, sports arenas, al fresco pushcarts, country fairs, church suppers, and beach-blanket barbecues.

It seems always within reach to be smeared on bread, dolloped onto the rim of a plate, dribbled from a foil pillow package, squeezed from a plastic bottle, pressed from a chrome counter pump, dabbed on a sliver of salami or a chunk of ham. These are the ways we know mustard best—but *not* how we should know it.

THE FLAVOR MAKER

Mustard is at its best, used as a cooking ingredient. It is a preeminent spice, a fact not understood by many American cooks. It is as important an ingredient in most of the world's great cuisines as pepper, paprika, oregano, basil, soy sauce, cinnamon, or a host of other spices.

Perhaps it fell into disrepute centuries ago because it was used to disguise the true flavor of rancid, rotten, or tainted food. Maybe it wasn't rare enough or expensive enough. Or perhaps because, if not used judiciously, it made everything taste alike, it was left to the diner rather than the cook to add the desired amount at the table instead of in the kitchen. In Britain and the U.S. its overwhelming use is as a condiment rather than as a seasoning.

Most of us are introduced to mustard at a very early age. It accompanies our first encounters with large crowds, and always evokes memories of amusement parks, sun, fun, and the fastest of fast foods, the hot dog.

DOG'S BEST FRIEND

Hot dogs, of course, are sausages, and sausages were eaten in Roman times. The Romans used ground meat mixed with spices. They stuffed the resultant combination into a casing, just as we do today. The hot dog as we know it, though, is not of Italian origin, but German. Or Austrian. It depends on which history book you read. In Vienna it is called a frankfurter. Perversely, in Frankfurt it is known as a wiener.

Its introduction to the U.S. market is variously credited to Charles Feltman or Antoine Feuchtwanger. Feltman apparently returned to New York from a visit to Germany in the late nineteenth century and opened a small restaurant in the resort of Coney Island. His restaurant sold, among other dishes, the smoked sausages he'd rediscovered on his trip abroad. A couple of years before the end of World War I, Nathan Handwerker, an employee of Feltman's, left that establishment and opened his own frankfurter stand. Nathan's Famous became a Coney Island landmark and now has been developed into a franchise operation that calls itself the world's largest purveyor of hot dogs.

More likely the first to popularize the hot dog in America was Bavarian-born Antoine Feuchtwanger, who introduced the novelty food at the St. Louis Exposition in 1904. He served it without a bun but with a mustard sauce. Parallel to Feuchtwanger's introduction of the hot dog, George and Francis French developed the first successfully manufactured prepared mustard in the U.S.—in Rochester, N.Y. Sales of both new products took off immediately.

RED-HOT SELLER

Harry M. Stevens, the concessionaire whose youthful vendors sold hot dogs off their backs from portable metal steamers at the old Polo Grounds in New York, invented the cry, "Red hots! Get your red hots!" It may have been he who first married the two great American pastimes, baseball and hot dogs.

Americans consume about 9 billion hot dogs a year, in one ball park or another. It takes a lot of mustard to coat 9 billion franks.

THE COWARDLY
YELLOW CONDIMENT

Ball-park mustard is usually a bright-yellow paste. It gets its brilliant color and flavor not from mustard, but from turmeric. Mustard's flavor is further subdued by vinegar and sugar. The taste and scorching heat of its namesake ingredient is hardly distinguishable.

This is the mustard Americans learn to love—or hate— from infancy. The fact that there are almost one hundred other foreign and domestic brands on grocery store shelves seems to matter little. Too exotic. Too far from the memories of childhood.

It's time to *unlearn* this flavor! It's time to save it for stadium fare. (At a tennis match held in a famous East Coast stadium recently, some spectators bought hot dogs that were immediately dubbed "haute dogs," because they were served with Dijon-style mustard in foil squeeze packs. The taste was wrong! Very un-American. Since tennis is a very classy sport, something chic, something "French" was invented by a P.R. person. The result insulted both products. Franco-American relations failed miserably with the frank.)

American mustard has its place as a condiment. But it should not be an ingredient in salad dressings or sauces, nor used with good beef, pork, or lamb. It does not enhance shrimp or delicate veal sausages. With some hamburgers, okay. With hot dogs, very definitely. As a cooking ingredient, no!

IMPORTED MUSTARDS

Except for Grey Poupon Dijon-style mustard made by Heublein in California, most mustards we recommend for cooking are imported. They are among the least expensive of gastronomic luxuries. Those found in the fancy-food sections of department stores, delicacy and specialty-food shops usually can be bought for about a dollar—unless you're a sucker for fancy packaging (an inexpensive gift, astonishingly expensive for cooking).

Prices for mustards vary tremendously, depending on

where you buy a specific brand or how elaborately it's packaged.

Packaging, however, does cost money, and if you're interested in the container, you'll pay a premium for it. If you're interested only in the contents, buy mustard in a no-frills package.

Distribution of even the most esoteric imported brands of Dijon is nationwide. If you like a particular kind that you've found in a fancy-food store, ask your local supermarket manager to stock it.

MUSTARD, THE
BREAD-AND-BUTTER GIFT

If you cook with mustard in great quantity, forget the fancy packaging. Spring for pretty pots only when you intend to refill them with a less costly version. Or if you want to bring something unusual to a hostess. An empty wine bottle gets tossed out; flowers wither and die. But a prettily decorated mustard pot can be refilled endlessly with mustard, pencils, spoons—or the flowers another guest brings.

As for the mustard itself, there are more and more kinds to choose from. Besides the old-standby American brands, there are twenty or more Dijon brands imported from France which range from mild to *extra forte*, the similar but much milder Dusseldorf and the sweet Bavarians from Germany, the classic English mustard powder from Colman, fiery Chinese, pungent Polish, sweetish Swedish, and any number of grainy and flavored mustards from France, including dark, sweet Bordeaux.

The neck-and-neck best sellers among the Dijons imported to the U.S., we are told, are Mâitre Jacques and France's own favorite, Amora. These two are followed closely by Maille and Pommery. After this quartet, the list is long and the tastes are varied. Some are saltier than others, some drier. Even among bottles of the same brand, you may find differences in strength. This has nothing to do with quality control, but with mustard's shelf life. Try to discover how long a particular jar you're contemplating buying has been in the store. Chances are, it's at least six to eight weeks out of the factory, at its freshest. If it stays on a store shelf, unrefrigerated, for several more months, it could lose some of its punch. Taste it before using it in a recipe. You may want to add more—or less—according to its strength. There will be nothing wrong with the mustard; it just may not be as strong as you like it.

THERE ARE
NO BAD MUSTARDS

Mustard, no matter what its age, will never "go bad." It won't grow mold, mildew, or harmful bacteria. A jar may not pack the wallop of its youth, it may have dried to almost a powder, its flavor may have weakened to utter blandness, it may even have darkened to a deep bronze color, but it can't harm you.

THE SLOW BURN

If you don't hold with store-bought and mix your own mustard, expect it to be a lot more ferocious than what you're used to spooning from a jar. An enzyme causes glucosides, those chemical relatives of sugar (glucose), to react with the water and release the heat most of us associate with the little dishes of the condiment served at Chinese restaurants (Chinese mustard is a combination of mustard powder and water, that's all). The heat, pungency, and bite are due to an essential oil which forms when the powder and liquid combine to form a paste. The burn is slow to develop; the paste should be allowed to rest for ten or fifteen minutes—to allow the heat to emerge full force. Other liquids such as vinegar and beer can be used, but they weaken the enzyme reaction and inhibit the pungency of the mixture. This milder result may be preferred, though, as with some French, German, and Polish mustards.

American mustards almost always lack sting. Manufacturers in this country do not heed Chaucer's admonition: "Woe to the cook whose sauces had no sting." Their products are lacking proportionately in mustard (they are made from less pungent *alba*, or white, seeds for starters) and are allowed to "age" for weeks before being bottled. Standing around puts out mustard's fire (ironically, water kindles it), which is why it is recommended by most producers of strong imported mustards to store the jar in the refrigerator once it is opened. Mixing with boiling water also makes a milder mustard—but because some of the glucosides are unconverted, this mustard will taste bitter.

After the essential oils have been activated and allowed to develop for ten or fifteen minutes, salt and vinegar may be added; they preserve strength rather than dissipate it.

Although the oils are volatile, mustard will not lose its pungency when added to a recipe during cooking if it is added near the end of the preparation time and the heat is kept down to a simmer. In cooked dishes, where the flavor of mustard is desired, but not the pungency, higher temperatures and longer cooking times will subdue it.

TO UNSTUFF
A STUFFED NOSE

Mustard's heat, unlike that produced by chili peppers, doesn't build in intensity as one eats more. At full, searing strength the sensation mustard causes travels instantaneously up through the sinuses, causing noses to run and eyes to tear.

When you have a stuffed nose, don't reach for a nasal spray; go to the kitchen cupboard for the can of Colman's dry mustard. Mix up a small batch, combining a teaspoonful of the powder with enough water to give it the consistency of heavy cream. Spread it thickly on a salted cracker and eat it in one or two bites. Clears out a stuffy nose in seconds (and the expense is negligible).

Hot mustard eaten with spare ribs or sausages as an appetizer will not in any way dull the appreciation of more delicately flavored foods that follow. The heat does not persist, but dissipates after each swallow. Mustard is a unique spice that can be used at the beginning, the middle, or the end of a meal and not adversely affect the enjoyment of accompanying dishes or beverages. As a matter of fact, small amounts of mustard, such as the quantities used in mayonnaise and other sauces, stimulate the taste buds. In this way mustard behaves like MSG (monosodium glutamate) but without giving you the Chinese Restaurant Syndrome.

IN A PICKLE

Mustard has been used as a good preservative and pickling spice since ancient times. It inhibits the growth of certain yeasts and discourages molds and bacteria from developing. It also adds its own piquant flavor to whatever you're pickling. The most commonly used seed is the white. It's bigger and bolder and is added whole to pickles, relishes, and condiments where the look of the whole seed is considered an aesthetic attraction. It is more strongly preservative than black or brown seeds.

Mustard has another interesting side effect—as an emulsifier. Enough of it in a salad dressing will hold the oil and vinegar together. In Hollandaise sauce it can minimize the threat of curdling. It not only helps prevent liquids from separating, but in its powdered form it absorbs one and a half times its weight in oil and twice its weight in vinegar.

THE FRATERNAL
MUSTARD TWINS

Mustard is so old, has been traded for so long, and is so easily cultivated in temperate climates, that its true origins are vague. It first blazed a culinary trail in Pakistan thousands of years ago. Curry was the vehicle. Not a spice in itself, but a mixture of powdered spices, curry usually contained ground mustard. The species used was *Brassica juncea*, known also as "brown" or "oriental" mustard seed. Brown and oriental seeds are slightly different in character but share the same chemical make-up. The average fixed oil in the oriental seed tends to be slightly higher than in the brown, which in turn is higher in protein and fiber. These fraternal twins average about 2 mm. in diameter. The brown seeds are reddish brown to dark brown in color, while the oriental seeds are for the most part light yellow, with occasional brownish ones intermingled. Unlike black and white mustards, these seeds contain a volatile oil which gives off a pungent aroma as well as a bite. Chinese restaurant mustard, hot English mustard, Dijon and German prepared mustards all have this same effect on the nose and mouth because all are made mostly from brown or oriental seeds.

The origins of *Brassica juncea* are disputed by botanical historians. It is claimed to have originated in Africa, Northern Europe, or the interior of China. It depends on whom you read. Wherever these types once came from, today they are widely cultivated. The U.S. draws most of its supply from Canada and the Dakotas. Dijon imports most of its brown seeds from these same sources. In the past few years, oriental seed seems to be replacing brown in North American growing regions.

WHITE MUSTARD

The seeds of *Brassica hirta Moench*, known as *alba* or "white" mustard, are slightly larger than the other types. They average about 3 mm. in diameter and are flattened laterally into a somewhat oval shape. Although called "white" (some call them yellow), they are a pale straw color—often with a pink blush. The major characteristic distinction of this seed is that its sharp taste burns but has no aromatic pungency.

Brassica hirta is thought to have originated in Europe. It is widely cultivated there, and the U.S. still imports it from Denmark and the United Kingdom. Those amounts are small, however, and we get most of what we need from Canada and the Dakota-Montana region.

BLACK MUSTARD

The third of the major types of mustard seed is "black" or *Brassica nigra*. *Brassica nigra* looks very much like brown mustard seed. It is about the same size, with a shape more round than oblong. This species is thought to be native to Europe and the Middle East. Until the end of World War II it was the main seed used commercially in Europe, but since then browns and orientals have replaced it because they can be grown and harvested more economically. The black mustard plant produces stalks eight to ten feet high, with a pod so brittle that machine harvesting is all but impossible. Mechanized farming breaks the pod, leaving most of the seed behind in the field. Because hand harvesting is too costly, black mustard is of no consequence in the American market. A small amount is still used in Europe and today is grown only in a few areas such as southern Italy, Sicily, Rumania, and Ethiopia, where it can be economically harvested with a sickle.

ON THE MUSTARD TRAIL

In addition to the Dakotas and Montana, Canada, Denmark, Ethiopia, Rumania, and Italy, mustard is also grown in California, Oregon, and Washington, and is a staple crop in Argentina, Australia, China, England, France, India, the Netherlands, Poland, Hungary, and the Soviet Union.

The hardy plant reproduces itself so easily that it has been considered a noxious weed. When the Spanish padres established the Mission Trail in California, they scattered mustard seeds like Hansel and Gretel scattered bread crumbs. In this manner they marked the way as they went from mission to mission. Unlike the unfortunate children in the fairy tale, though, birds did not gobble up what the friars had left behind, and the plants flourished. The well-marked paths were easy to find, and these mustard trails can still be traced in the vicinity of some California missions.

Mustard plants produce bright-yellow flowers, each with six stamens and four petals which create a cross characteristic of the mustard family; their Latin name, *Cruciferae*, means "cross bearer." In our western states the flowers of the crop are important to the honey industry. In the Lampoc Valley of Santa Barbara County, California, swarms of bees feast on mustard nectar, producing large quantities of mild-flavored, light-colored honey. It has no hint of mustard flavor.

White mustard, besides being grown for its seed, may be grown as a cover crop or as "green manure"—a crop plowed under when only half grown, to add rich organic matter to the soil. It is used as a salad plant in kitchen gardens and window boxes and sprouted (like alfalfa and beans). These pungent sprouts are marvelous sprinkled over tomatoes (page 185) or put in a sandwich instead of lettuce or watercress.

If you're into sprouting other seeds and beans, use your

11

favorite germinating method with mustard seeds. The results are quick and rewarding.

As field crops, the mustards are fast-growing and do not require much rainfall. They must mature during dry weather, however. White performs best in heavy, sandy loam, while the black/brown does better in a lighter soil. The seeds are planted in the spring, the darker seeds earlier than the light, at about four pounds to the acre for the latter and three pounds for the former. Both seeds should be harvested before the mature pods open because the pods burst as soon as they are ripe, scattering seeds for the next year's crop. White mustard pods are rough to the touch and hairy, while the darker species have narrow, smooth, elongated pods.

THE FRENCH CONNECTION

"Dijon" is the generic term for a style of mustard produced in this picturesque city in eastern France. It is situated on the western border of the fertile plain of Burgundy, of which province it was once the capital. Dijon is the gateway to the Burgundy wine country to the south.

It is a culinary capital also famous for *pain d'épices,* or gingerbread, and cassis—black-currant syrup.

Other noted gastronomic treasures from Dijon include vinegar, brandy, beer, flour, candy, jelly, and cookies. An adventure awaits travelers who happen to be in the city in November for the *Foire Gastronomique.*

Dijon is the birthplace of two exclusive gastronomic orders: the Order of the *Chevaliers du Tastevin* and the *Toison d'Or* (Golden Fleece).

Standing on a downtown corner at rue de la Liberté, 32, is the Grey Poupon store, which looks like an old apothecary because of its somber black facade. Its glass windows are lined with antique ceramic mustard pots decorated with birds, leaves, flowers, and French and Latin inscriptions.

Inside are more shelves containing arrays of ancient and new *moutardiers*. The old pots are not for sale, but the new ones are. Choose one and it is spirited away to the back of the shop to be filled, gratis, with a strong, wonderfully aromatic Dijon mustard. This potent white-wine-based brew is the shop's best seller, but others, flavored with various herbs and seasonings, are gaining favor. They can be purchased there in anything from foil packets to two-and-a-half-pound buckets. Grey Poupon (founded in 1777) vends vinegars, spices, condiments, and mustards by Maille and Parizot. Maille, now owned by Grey Poupon, is even older than its parent company. Founded in 1747, it was once located in Paris and was purveyor to the infamous Mme. de Pompadour. Originally a vinegar maker, Maille was given the title of Vinegar Distiller to the King of France, and manufactured for the emperors of Germany and Russia.

The Real Thing

Only mustards produced in Dijon may be lawfully labeled Dijon. Others may be designated as Dijon-style. Heublein's Grey Poupon brand made in California is the only one outside the territorial limits that is licensed to use the name Dijon. Although good, it is not the same in taste or strength as the French Grey Poupon. That brand is not sold in this country.

Up to the seventeenth century, dry mustard was made in Dijon, which by then had become an important center for merchants of the world's spices. The powder was compressed into bricks, tablets, or pellets, which were mixed with liquids and spices. In 1634 the vinegar and mustard manufacturers of Dijon, at their own request, were given exclusive right to make mustard. They had various obligations under the legislation; their workers had to wear "clean and modest clothes," conduct themselves properly, own only one shop in town, and mark their names on all casks and stone jars. Seeds were ground by hand; workers who shed the most tears received a bonus for their finer powder.

Typical modern Dijons are creamy, smooth, and pale yellow. When fresh they are strong and assertive enough to make tears flow. All Dijons are made from dark mustard seeds which are ground and sifted to remove the hulls and then mixed with partly fermented white wine or vinegar. In France, only mustards made with dark mustard seeds may be labeled *moutarde*. Mustard and mustard products made with the pale-yellow or white seeds (most American and German brands) must be called *condiment*.

Today, Unrefined Is Refined

Moutarde à l'Ancien is enjoying a vogue here. This product is like mustards were before eighteenth-century innovations removed the hulls. Although often more expensive to buy, *Moutarde à l'Ancien* is actually cheaper to manufacture since it does not require the sifting process and leaves the hulls in the flour. This chewier product is analogous to chunky peanut butter in its style. The taste is gentler than that of a mustard made from powder alone because the hulls contain little of the powerful enzyme released when the seeds are ground. If the seeds are soaked in vinegar before grinding, the result is even milder.

The foremost brand of the coarse-grained *l'ancien*-style products sold in the U.S. is *Moutarde de Meaux Pommery*, a.k.a. the Abbot's Mustard. This very mustard was served, it is said, at the tables of French kings beginning in 1632. Brillat-Savarin called it the mustard for gourmets and said, in great promotional style: "If it isn't Meaux, it isn't mustard."

All in all, the mustard-making process is a simple one, requiring at the most a half hour of factory time, from grinding to storage, before packaging. Dijon is made essentially the same way, whether it is manufactured in gleaming automated factories or by small private firms. The oldest factory, in continuous operation for almost 130 years, is that of *Theveniaud*, at Villars, just outside Dijon. The ground seeds are mixed with salt, water, and vinegar in big wooden vats. The hulls are strained off after the mustard emerges as a paste. Later the paste is mixed with wine and seasonings in other wooden vats and left to age.

French Favorite

Amora is the most prestigious Dijon mustard producer in France. During a normal day, over 115 tons of mustard are packaged at *Amora's* three plants—about 300,000 jars, tubes, and tins. This translates into gross annual sales of $150 million. Hot cakes, move over!

As you can see, Frenchmen consume a lot more mustard than Americans do, about .74 kilos (1.63 pounds) per capita every year (85 percent of it made in Dijon). Under more than eighty labels they manufacture two-thirds of the world's supply of French mustard in Burgundy—more than 49,000 tons. By contrast, Americans only use about half a pound per person, and that is mostly American ball-park mustard.

Where does the rest of French mustard come from? Bordeaux. Bordeaux mustard is frowned upon by the Dijonnais, and not only because it takes away some of their business. It is a much darker-colored mixture (it contains the seed coat and red wine vinegar), is sweet in taste (due to an abundance of sugar), and flavored with lots of tarragon and other herbs and spices. In Dijon they say Bordeaux mustard is "coarse, crude, lacks any subtlety, and is fit only for sausages and Englishmen." Bordeaux is milder than Dijon, lacks its clean, pungent taste, and is not recommended for cooking. It is, however, very nice with sausages and ham, especially on sandwiches.

In England, where mustard is "hot as blazes," French mustard often meant the dark Bordeaux type because shipments of it accompanied French wines which came from this important port. "Consequently," some Burgundians say, "the English were not only deprived of our best wines, but our best mustard as well." Bordeaux mustard, like that from Germany and Sweden, has its uses—primarily as a condiment with cold meats and the aforementioned sausages. It is rarely used as a flavoring in cooking.

HAIL, CAESAR!

If mustard is one of the epicurean splendors of Burgundy, Burgundians can thank the Romans for bringing it to the region in the first place. Caesar's conquering legions sowed mustard seed in the hills around Dijon. It has been manufactured there ever since the fourth century, when the local vinegar makers were authorized to use the secret formula for mustard devised by Palladius, son of Exuperantius, Prefect of the Gauls.

Palladius's recipe directed: "Reduce twelve pints of mustard seed to powder. Add a pound of honey, a pound of Spanish oil, a pint of strong vinegar. Blend thoroughly and use." Not exactly the Dijon we know and love today.

Garum, that famous and all-pervasive Roman seasoning which Apicius used in almost every sauce, often contained mustard—but no more than one-tenth by volume. Garum was composed of fish intestines, gills, and other offal, steeped in a thick brine laced with various ingredients such as pepper, vinegar, wine, water, oil, mushrooms, mint, raisins, honey, and so on. The vessel containing this mixture was set uncovered in the sun to ferment. It was stirred from time to time and the almost-liquid pulp which resulted after two or three months was strained and the sauce, bottled. As Pliny relates, it sold for as much as or more than the most precious perfumes.

Garum sounds dreadful, yet if we analyzed some of our own table sauces, such as Worcestershire or anchovy sauce, perhaps we would be equally repulsed.

THE REAL CRADLE

Man first thought to plant seeds in 8000 B.C. Two thousand years later, in the valley of the Indus River, a civilization blossomed even earlier than that in what is usually considered the "cradle of civilization," the valleys of the Tigris and Euphrates rivers.

The Mesapotamians, Sumerians, Chaldeans, and Babylonians got their first lemon and orange seeds from these people of the Indus Valley. Even the Chinese, it is thought, got their first grains of rice from this civilization 5000 years ago.

Inhabitants of these ancient cities cooked food in sesame oil and were the first to season their foods with mustard. The Chinese may have gotten mustard seeds from the Indus Valley. Though he does not mention its origins, the Chinese Emperor Shen Nung, nearly 5000 years ago, listed mustard in his ancient herbal. The Chinese apparently cultivated mustard in those early times and used it both medicinally and for seasoning.

Egyptian papyri dating to 2800 B.C. record the medicinal uses of mustard. Mustard seeds have been found in the Great Pyramids and in the tombs discovered in the Valley of the Kings. The Egyptians seasoned meat by popping a few mustard seeds into their mouths as they chewed, thus being the first to use mustard as a condiment.

MUSTARD GETS AROUND

How did mustard seed find its way to Greece and Rome in the first place? Even to Egypt? It wasn't indigenous to the Mediterranean peninsula or the Nile Valley. At the time most Eastern luxuries had been brought to these sophisticated ancient cultures by those early traveling salesmen and monopolists, the Arabs. The Arabs controlled the overland trade routes to and from southern Arabia and Asia. The seafaring Phoenicians were also involved, taking cargoes of spices and cloth from Arab ports on the eastern shores of the Mediterranean to Spain and up the Atlantic coast.

Growing populations of the first great civilizations, however, with their voracious appetite for spices, could not afford to rely on the somewhat capricious commerce of the past, nor could they afford to go on paying the exorbitant prices extorted from them by the Arabs. Romans had to find some way to break the Arab monopoly, not only to appease their treasuries, but their palates as well. They did find a solution—if only temporarily. First they built ships large enough to navigate the waters between Egyptian Red Sea ports and India, and so fetch their own spices. Then they spread, through the agency of their invading legions and settlers, the growth of any plants and herbs which would "take" in their imperial outposts.

Mustard was one seed which would grow almost anywhere from North Africa to Great Britain. And it did. It was naturalized in fields around settlements and by the sides of roads. Along with mustard, the Romans planted savory, dill, rosemary, garlic, parsley, thyme, and mint. These herbs and mustard have been in continuous cultivation in northern Europe ever since.

THE SUN SETS ON ROME

When Rome fell, a curtain fell over Europe and the Dark Ages began. The Roman sea route to India became unstable; the vessels, the prey of pirates and robbers. The camel caravans that traveled the land routes now found few outlets for their spices and sumptuous silks. Rome had drained the West of precious metals and gold. The treasury was in ruin, and so when Rome collapsed, international trade collapsed as well, and the barter economy of a thousand years before prevailed again. Northern Europe carried on little trade after the Romans left; most southern trade routes were blocked by raiding barbarians. Its economy, such as it was, was constantly disrupted by war and invasion.

It was only in southern Europe that the spice trade continued—to a very limited extent. Venice became a natural trading center. A few Venetian galleys loaded with spices transported their cargoes to countries surrounding the Mediterranean from Constantinople, the westernmost outpost of the ancient overland spice routes. The traders returned with holds crammed with salt and salted meats for the Byzantine Empire. Spices, at least the Asian varieties, were still prohibitively expensive.

It wasn't until the great Muslim Empire enveloped the Mediterranean and spread into North Africa and Spain toward the end of the eighth century that the spice trade increased again.

Imperial Seeds

Mustard, because it was easily cultivated and available almost everywhere (the Caliphs introduced it to Spain during the Arab occupation of the Iberian peninsula), became one of the most esteemed seasonings of the Middle Ages, brightening an otherwise drab cuisine.

By the ninth century, mustard was grown on convent grounds near Paris and sold to provide revenue for the church. Charlemagne, the first ruler to bear the title Holy Roman Emperor and a diligent scholar deeply interested in horticulture, decreed in 812 that the spice be grown on all imperial farms in central Europe. Besides using the seeds as a seasoning and preservative, the leaves were eaten alone, added to the cauldron, or used as a salad green.

With the Norman invasion of England in 1066, a revolution began in cooking—at least in the British Isles. The Normans brought with them a more sophisticated palate. A renewal of foreign trade, increased freedom of movement in the western world, numerous wars and invasions of foreign cultures helped develop a more complex menu distinguished by a rebirth of interest in spices.

Crusading for Better Cooking

A half century later, the start of the Crusades intermingled cultures still further, and crusaders returned home with new ideas about cooking, spices, and living standards. This was especially apparent in Britain. A pepperhorn became essential in the kitchen of even the tiniest English farmstead. In the wealthiest households mustard was too common, too accessible, we suppose, to remain as important an ingredient as it had been for hundreds of years and was supplanted, to an extent, by ginger, cloves, mace, pepper, and many other spices newly imported from the Moluccas (or Spice Islands) and other areas of Asia.

Mustard became an important crop in Germany in the twelfth century. Comparatively inexpensive, it was the "poor man's spice," along with cumin, coriander, fennel, and caraway.

The Crusades had helped to refine cooking techniques. New raw materials were introduced. Crusaders returned with more sophisticated palates. Dishes became lavishly spiced, not just to disguise the flavor of meat and fish which were "high." Spices had this effect, of course, but were necessary to help digest tough salted and dried meats and to act as a disinfectant and preservative.

Beat It!

One of the staples of the Middle Ages household was stockfish with mustard, especially as a Lenten food. It needed a strong arm to prepare it, a requisite to which a writer of the period testifies: "And when . . . it is desired to eat it, it behoves to beat it with a wooden hammer for a full hour, and then set it to soak in warm water for a full two hours or more, then cook and scour it well like beef; then eat it with mustard. . . ."

In poorer homes food would be seasoned with pepper, garlic, fennel, peony, and mustard seeds. In affluent households and in those of the feudal lords, more exotic spices from the East strongly seasoned everything that was put on the table. Even dishes as simple as porridge sometimes contained a half dozen spices. And in one recipe for fresh strawberries, their fresh flavor was drowned in pepper, ginger, saffron, galingale (a strong, hot gingerlike root with the aroma of roses), vinegar, and alkanet root (a potent red dye). It seems medieval man was suspicious of fresh fruit and the taste of it was unwelcome, especially when it could so easily be changed by the addition of spices.

The craze for spices was odd, given the fact that the costs were so high that even in the wealthiest homes they were put under lock and key, hidden in strongboxes, special cupboards, and safes. Although not quite as emphatically seasoned, the only cooking that survives today which is similar to that of medieval Europe is the food of the Middle East, which combines meats, fruits, grains, aromatics, and spices in one dish.

MUSKETEERS
NEED NOT APPLY

By the thirteenth century the occupation of "mustarder" was common in England. These individual entrepreneurs used two small millstones (querns) to grind the seed. Smaller versions were used in kitchens and on sideboards. Mustard was also crushed in hand mills, just as pepper is today.

Mustarders usually steeped the crushed seeds in vinegar

and sold it in glass or earthenware pots closed with parchment torn from old records and documents. Decanted from this commercial packaging, mustard sauces were carried to the table in small, shallow metal vessels, kept separate from other similar bowls because of the corrosive action of the vinegar on the metals.

Nepotism

The most famous mustarder of the fourteenth century was a nephew of Pope John XXII. Pope John loved mustard so much, he is reputed to have put it on almost everything he ate. Not knowing what to do with an incorrigible nephew "who roamed back alleys, was as stupid as a sturgeon, and vain as Narcissus," he appointed him *Premier Moutardier du Pape*. The appointment not only kept the boy out of trouble but gave rise to the expression "mustard maker to the Pope," which is still applied to a person of extreme vanity and stupidity.

UNFAIR FARE

Spices were the status symbols of the fourteenth century. The more heavily laden with spices the food served at his table, the richer the man was supposed to be. The only difference between the food of the rich and the poor was that the food of the rich would be pungent with ginger, cinnamon, cloves, and pepper, while the food of the poor was redolent of garlic, leeks, onions, and black and white mustard seeds.

Spice Supports

Spices still performed the function of making spoiled meat taste better and of giving character to the insipid salted and dried foods of winter (more character than was really necessary). They also became a sort of currency: a pound of pepper represented the equivalent of two or three week's wages for a laborer.

Throughout the Dark Ages spices were so prized that they were used as part of royal dowries and to pay magistrates. They were listed in the inventories of castles and among the possessions of prominent people. They were tributes to kings, inspirations to poets. Despite their scarcity and inflated prices, they were consumed in greater quantity per capita than they are today, according to the French historian Pierre Gaxotti. The poor stuck to mustard and other home-grown herbs, while the rich had the wherewithal to afford the luxury of spices.

In royal households at least one servant, formerly the mustarder, now the "Yoeman Powder Beater," had the job of grinding spices for everyday meals and banquets. After dinner, plates of more spices were passed in wealthy homes, much as Indians and Pakistanis are offered *paandaans*—compartmented brass or silver boxes holding spices, nuts, and betel leaves—to round off a meal and give a feeling of well-being. Others carried spices with them to eat like candy or refresh and scent their mouths—just like today's breath fresheners, mouthwashes, and chewing gums.

CUTTING OUT
THE MIDDLEMAN

The lure of riches to be made from spices and the European vow to break the intolerable monopoly of the Arab-Venetian middlemen on the spice trade from Constantinople, Damascus, and Alexandria, combined with two other developments in the fifteenth century to inspire Columbus to seek an overseas route to India and the Spice Islands to buy directly from the producers.

The overland spice routes from the East were constantly being disrupted by Turkish wars in Asia Minor. This made the supply of spices sporadic and the price higher than ever.

The second development was ship design. In the 1420s Henry the Navigator pioneered the invention of a sturdy three-masted (instead of single-masted) merchant ship which could withstand the open seas, make headway against trade winds, and make the use of supplementary oars unnecessary.

Fame, the desire to establish the church among the heathen, and economic necessity sent Columbus on his way. He landed in the "Indies" in 1492 but found none of the glittering cities and powerful kingdoms which he had expected.

In 1498 Vasco da Gama found a successful route to India around the Cape of Good Hope. Like carrying coals to Newcastle, da Gama carried mustard in his provisions. He returned from the Malabar coast with cloves, cinnamon, ginger, and pepper. Portugal now controlled the spice traffic. Within twenty-five years the nations of Europe would complain that their treasuries were being robbed by the Portuguese, just as they had been by the Venetians and Arabs before them. Although Magellan soon discovered a western route to the Spice Islands around South America, the Portuguese continued to control the spice trade for another century.

A New World of Food

Columbus did not bring back valuable cargoes of spices but he inadvertently opened up a world of new foods, tastes, and textures to Europeans: corn, turkey, peanuts, cashews, black walnuts, cocoa, vanilla, potatoes, sweet potatoes, tomatoes, several kinds of beans, squashes, bell peppers, pimiento, allspice, chili peppers, paprika, cayenne, pineapple, and papaya all came from the New World. Food also traveled in the other direction. New colonists brought seeds and seedlings. Mustard was one of them.

In the seventeenth century the Dutch finally broke the Portuguese spice monopoly. Within a few years the East India Company, established by eighty London merchants in 1599, finally made England self-sufficient in terms of spices. Because the English were heavy meat eaters and meat tended to spoil quickly, spices were important to this cuisine. As in ancient Rome, cooks in Britain were often judged by their skill in disguising foods.

This style of eating changed drastically in Europe and England during the 1600s, with the introduction of cheaper spices and sugar. Spices became less popular as they became cheaper, losing their glamour along with their exclusivity.

THE ORIGINAL
NOUVELLE CUISINE

La Varenne's revolutionary cookbooks were published about midcentury and the *nouvelle cuisine* of the seventeenth century was launched. Vegetables were lightly seasoned, meats were served with their natural juices, light sauces were simply flavored with herbs and lemon juice. The natural flavors of foods began to emerge—and to be enjoyed. Cheap West Indian sugar turned European cooking away from the use of excessive spices; cooking styles as we know them today began to develop. Mustard, a vital ingredient in many medieval recipes, turned into a condiment served at the table—especially in England.

The Old Ball Game

Mustard in Shakespeare's England was usually bought from vendors in the form of mustard balls. Tewkesbury was its most famous place of manufacture. The seeds were crushed and pounded, mixed with peaseflour (remember "pease porridge hot, pease porridge cold" . . . ?), moistened with water, and pressed into balls and mixed with vinegar, grape or apple juice, cider, red wine, buttermilk, cherry juice, or other fruit juice. Honey might be added.

Conspicuous Consumption

The Tudors were great consumers of mustard. In the household of the Earl of Northumberland, 160 to 190 gallons of made-mustard were used every year. His Household Book, started in 1512, stipulated that "whereas Mustard hath been bought of the Sauce-maker afore time that now it be made within my Lord's house and that one be provided to be Groom of the Scullery that can make it." The mustarder got a new title.

In *The Queen-Like Closet or Rich Cabinet*, in 1670, Hannah Wooley recommended sieving the crushed mustard seed after pounding. "To make the best sort mustard: Dry well your seed, then beat by little and little at a time in a Mortar, and sift it, then put the powder in a Gally pot, and wet it with vinegar very well, then put in a whole Onion pilled but not cut, a little Pepper beaten, a little Salt, and a lump of stone sugar."

THE POWER BEHIND
THE POWDER

Not until 1720, did a commercial method evolve for separating the hulls from the rest of the seed. This method was invented by a Mrs. Clements of Durham, England. Mrs. Clements's mustard was a dry, pale-yellow flour, very fine in texture and better in appearance than any milled before it. She produced it by grinding the seeds on small millstones, then removed the hulls by putting the ground seeds through ever-finer sieves. Known as Durham Mustard, the powder quickly won the approval of the royal family and was sought after throughout the British Isles. Durham, rather than Tewkesbury, became the center of mustard production. When King George III visited Tewkesbury in 1788 and asked about mustard balls, they had long since disappeared.

A Legend in Her Own Time

In 1807 a London publication, the *Gentleman's Magazine*, turned Mrs. Clements into a legend:

> There are probably but few individuals now living acquainted with the history of the manufacture of Durham Mustard. Prior to 1720 there was no such luxury as mustard in its present form at our tables. At that time the seed was only coarsely pounded in a mortar, as coarsely separated from the integument, and in that rough state prepared for use. In the year I have mentioned, it occurred to an old woman of the name of Clements, resident at Durham, to grind the seed in a mill, and to pass the meal through the various processes which are resorted to in making flour from wheat. The secret she kept for many years to herself, and in the period of her exclusive possession of it, supplied the principal parts of the kingdom, and in particular the metropolis, with this article; and George the First stamped it with fashion by his approval. Mrs. Clements as regularly as twice a year travelled to London, and the principal towns throughout England, for orders, as any tradesman's rider of the present day; and the old lady continued to pick up not only a decent pittance, but what was then thought a tolerable competency. From this woman's residing at Durham, it acquired the name Durham Mustard.

Mrs. Clements's method of making mustard flour is still used today (with variations) for mustard production.

Mustard also had its detractors. In 1640 John Parkinson wrote of mustard: "Our ancient forefathers, even the better sort, were not sparing in the use thereof . . . but nowadays it is seldom used by their successors, being accounted the clownes sauces and therefore not fit for their table."

Quality Control

In spite of Parkinson, England continued to consume huge quantities of the stuff. In the second half of the seventeenth century Sir Hugh Plat complained that the British had some of the same problems with its mustard processors as those that had caused the French in 1634 to legislate quality standards for the manufacture of Dijon. He noted in his *Delightes for Ladies*: "Our mustard which we buy from the Chandlers at this day is many times made up with vile and filthy vinegar, such as our stomak would abhore if we should see it before the mixing thereof with the seeds."

Mustard Spreads

Mustard flour as made in Durham jumped the Channel. The process found its way to almost every country that consumed mustard or manufactured the paste. It soon became the basic method for milling the powder used in making Dijon, Bordeaux, and German mustards.

Mrs. Clements had competitors. Her secret could not be kept for long. In 1723 this advertisement appeared in the London Journal:

To all FAMILIES, etc.—The Royal Flower of Mustard Seed is now used and esteemed by most of the Quality and Gentry. It will keep good in the Flower as long as in the seed, and one spoonful of the Mustard made of it will go as far as three of that sold at chandler's shops, and is much wholesomer. The Author (who may be heard of at the 'Maiden-Head' in Bow Church Yard) hath just invented a new Method of making it. Those who make Use of the Flower prepared by others, must be sure to remember what they are to have for dinner on the morrow, and mix their Flower over Night, and then it will hardly do by next day Noon; whereas the Mustard made of this Flower will be fit to eat in 15 minutes. Merchants, Captains of ships, and others, may be supplied wholesale at the place above said; sold also under the Dutch Church in Austin Fryars . . . Price 6 d. a Paper. Allowance to those who sell it again.

By 1742 the brothers Keen had established a mustard-making factory at Garlick Hill, London. Their factory prospered for well over a century, until it was absorbed by that other family dynasty, Colman's, in 1903.

THE PRESIDENT
SETS A PRECEDENT

Thomas Jefferson was born in Virginia one year after the Keens opened their London factory. Jefferson had a special interest in farming, gardening, food, and wines. As Minister to France at the Court of Louis XVI in the late 1780s, he became so enamored of French cuisine that Patrick Henry, a fellow-Virginian, once complained that Jefferson, on his return to the States, was "so Frenchified that he abjured his native victuals." Jefferson was worldly, inquisitive, and eclectic in his eating habits—and so, unjustly accused by Henry. He ate what he liked, and imported what he could not grow or raise around Monticello. While in Paris he had searched the markets and kitchens for superior products and ingredients. He collected recipes for favorite dishes and sauces to be prepared by his French chef.

Because the exporting of rice was forbidden, he risked the death penalty for smuggling out of Italy a strictly-guarded special strain of rice which would grow in dry fields. He collected hundreds of plants and seeds in his travels, for planting at Monticello, thus introducing them to America.

Jefferson stretched the boundaries of what was allowed his office and his position in American political life by having European food products brought to him in the diplomatic pouch from Paris, thus skirting tariffs, duties, and agricultural regulations. One product from abroad which was constantly on his list of "necessary" culinary items was French mustard. There is a recipe in the *Thomas Jefferson Cook Book* for wild turkey wings, crumbed, broiled, then baked with a mustard sauce.

IN THE BEGINNING
THERE WAS JEREMIAH

Jeremiah Colman, an English flour miller, began milling mustard in Norwich in 1814. On May 7 of that year this ad appeared in the *Norfolk Chronicle:*

> Jeremiah Colman—having taken the stock and trade lately carried on by Mr. Edward Ames, respectfully informs his customers and the Public in general, that he will continue the manufacturing of mustard. And he begs leave to assure those who may be pleased to favor him with their orders, that they shall be supplied in such a manner as cannot fail to secure their approbation.

This was the birth announcement of what was to become a British institution—of the kind the word "venerable" was coined for.

Company Town

In forty years the company grew so big that Jeremiah James—old Jeremiah's grandnephew, who had followed his father into the business—bought a large site in Carrow, Norwich, in 1854, and built a complex of factory buildings there. Expansion at the new location increased the workforce from two hundred to over a thousand by 1874. J.J.

and his wife, Caroline, were dedicated to the welfare of their workers and introduced social benefits that, for their time, were wholly unique: they employed a factory nurse, provided workers with cheap, nourishing meals fifty years before staff cafeterias became the norm, subsidized a school for workers' children, provided sports and recreational facilities and housing. The company has prospered in Norwich ever since, making the name Colman synonymous with mustard.

During the reign of Queen Victoria, Colman's enlarged its trade and sent its mustard all over the British Empire. Thousands of tons left the Carrow works every year, and by the 1880s Colman's had established branches in the U.S., India, Australia, and South America.

In 1866 Colman's was conferred a "Special Warrant as Manufacturer of Mustard to Her Majesty" by Queen Victoria. Appointment as "Purveyors of Mustard to The Royal Houses of Europe" followed quickly. By 1870 Colman's was supplying the Queen of Holland, Emperor Napoleon III of France, and the King of Italy.

A Christmas Tradition

Each year from the 1880s until 1939, Colman produced special mustard tins for the Christmas market in England. They held four, five, or six pounds of mustard. When empty they came in handy for storing tea, buttons, cookies, and money. Victorian households usually bought whole tinsful. But retailers also sold mustard from these tins in small papers. The designs on the tins were rich with illustrations showing royal events, colonial landmarks, new battleships, military commanders, and great British heroes.

Colman's also published beautifully illustrated children's booklets which it gave away every Christmas from the 1880s right up until the 1950s. They were inscribed with Christmas greetings to its young friends all over the world from J & J Colman, Ltd. The subject matter covered favorite fairytales, excerpts from literary classics, comic stories, rhymes, and songs, under such titles as *Mustard-ventures on Mars*, *The Mustard Pot Merry-Go-Round 1930*, *Mustard Pots' Race*, *Mustard Man Ready*, *The Magic Mustard Pot*, and *Tommy at the Court of King Colman*.

The Mustard Club

Colman's began one of its most popular and long-lived advertising campaigns in 1926 with the odd and comic adventures of the officers of a ficticious club, *The Mustard Club*, whose secret password was "Pass the mustard, please!" These officers advocated the wildest and most improbable uses for Colman's. There was a *Mustard Club Recipe Book* written by the famous English mystery writer Dorothy L. Sayers. Colman's issued badges and offered tobacco containers, as well as many other novelty items now sought after by collectors.

There's Nothing Colman's Can't Do

Colman's had a column in its Club bulletin called "*Mustard Uses Mustered*," which straightfacedly listed ways to use mustard not necessarily connected with the kitchen:

1) Make a paste and spread on back of tile to secure loose one to wall; 2) Use as fertilizer for better colored daffodils; 3) Sprinkle dry mustard inside shoes to prevent cold feet; 4) Mustard and honey at bedtime for coughs, a pinch of mustard in a wineglass of water for hiccoughs; 5) Colman's poultry mustard fed to chickens to stimulate egg production; 6) To mend leaky car radiators temporarily, pour in contents of 2 oz. tin of mustard while car is running; 7) Sprinkle dry mustard over plants to rid them of insect pests; 8) Two teaspoons in a pint of water poured on roots stops worms;

9) Dry mustard rubbed into dog's coat helps stop distemper. Cover dog with blanket; 10) Smear headlights with "made mustard" to drive in fog—fog lights.

The Colman Calmer

Colman's advertising department was created in 1880 and promoted such ideas as the mustard bath. The vogue for these baths began in the Victorian era as a pleasant restorative for the upper classes after the hunt or a ball. Colman's issued a special dispenser which looked like a big confectioner's-sugar sprinkler so even those without servants could enjoy the benefits of such a bath.

As late as 1927, an English food writer, in a book ingeniously entitled, *A Book of Food*, calls Britain's "water-made mustard" a "piteously amateur business, thin as buttermilk," and without flavor. He suggests that mustard powder "be banished from every self-respecting English home. . . . Recently some of our leading mustard-manufacturers have devoted considerable publicity to demonstrating the hygienic properties of mustard baths. This seems to be a far more rational use for mustard powder than the cauterization of our tongues." No Anglophile, the author finds French mustards "gracious, deliciously mild and suave . . . piquant and stimulating . . . warming . . . subtle." Colman's seems to have survived the criticism, its growth continuing, until today it is part of a world-wide trading organization, Reckitt & Colman, which long ago acquired the R. T. French Company of Rochester, N.Y., as U.S. agents, manufacturers, and distributors.

AS AMERICAN AS FRENCH

R. T. French manufactures ball-park mustard in Rochester. Their address is 1 Mustard Street. French's, like all the other American mustards, is made by first separating the useful seeds from pebbles, dust, stems, broken seeds, and weed seeds that the combine has also harvested. This is accomplished by using sieves and low-pressure air streams. The seeds are then weighed into batches, mixed with vinegar, water, turmeric (lots of it), and spices, and crushed into a slurry. The slurry is then pumped to a battery of high-speed stone mills and milled to the recognizable bright-yellow paste. The paste is collected in large holding tanks and then pumped to bottling machines, where it is put into jars, the labels are put on, and the jars packed in shipping cases.

Made from the white *alba* seeds, American mustards like French's are hot when fresh and have little true mustard taste (remember, the *alba* seeds burn but have almost no mustard flavor). "It must be aged and undergo flavor development in the jar," French's says. "During this aging period (about two weeks), the mustard develops its flavor, loses its heat, and becomes the product everyone enjoys on their hot dogs."

Powdered mustard is used by other food processors in the U.S. as an essential ingredient in mayonnaise, salad dressings, spice blends, hot dogs, sausages, potted meat spreads, barbecue sauces, and other food items. The oil from mustard seeds is used in other industries, chiefly in the manufacture of marine lubricants, high-pressure lubricants, and rolling oils in manufacturing light-gauge steel. It is also used in the production of nylon and plastic.

BY THE BOOK

Since the probable discovery of mustard in Pakistan millenniums ago, the spice has found its way to the hearts and stomachs of countless millions all over the world. It has been immortalized in the Bible and by Shakespeare and other literary giants. Anatole France, in *La Revolte des*

Anges, wrote: "A tale without love is like beef without mustard; an insipid dish." Boswell reported that "Johnson's conversation was much too strong for a person accustomed to obsequiousness and flattery; it was mustard in a young child's mouth." Shakespeare immortalized Tewkesbury mustard when he had Falstaff exclaim in *Henry IV:* "His wit's as thick as Tewkesbury mustard!"

Lewis Carroll has Alice discuss mustard when she meets the Duchess after wandering off during that curious croquet match:

> ". . . flamingos and mustard both bite (said the Duchess). And the moral of that is—'Birds of a feather flock together.' "
>
> "Only mustard isn't a bird," Alice remarked.
>
> "Right, as usual," said the Duchess. "What a clear way you have of putting things!"
>
> "It's a mineral, I *think*," said Alice.
>
> "Of course it is," said the Duchess, who seemed ready to agree to everything that Alice said. "There's a large mustard mine near here. And the moral of that is—'The more there is of mine, the less there is of yours.' "
>
> "Oh, I know!" exclaimed Alice, who had not attended to this last remark. "It's a vegetable. It doesn't look like one, but it is."

You're getting warm, Alice.

The Bible makes several references to the size of mustard seeds, comparing them to heaven and faith. In Matthew:

> Another parable put he forth unto them, saying, The kingdom of heaven is like to a grain of mustard seed, which a man took, and sowed in his field: Which indeed is the least of all seeds: but when it is grown, it

is the greatest among herbs, and becometh a tree, so that the birds of the air come and lodge in the branches thereof.

In Mark:

And he said, Whereunto shall we liken the kingdom of God? or with what comparison shall we compare it? It is like a grain of mustard seed, which, when it is sown in the earth, is less than all the seeds that be in the earth: But when it is sown, it groweth up, and becometh greater than all others, and shooteth out great branches; so that the fowls of the air may lodge under the shadow of it.

In Luke:

Then said he, Unto what is the kingdom of God like? and whereunto shall I resemble it? It is like a grain of mustard seed, which a man took, and cast into his garden; and it grew, and waxed a great tree; and the fowls of the air lodged in the branches of it.

And again on faith, in Matthew:

If ye have faith as a grain of mustard seed, ye shall say unto this mountain, Remove hence to yonder place; and it shall remove; and nothing shall be impossible unto you.

A common French phrase says: "C'est de la Moutarde après dîner,"—it's like putting mustard on the table after dinner has been eaten—which means that something arrives too late to be useful.

A Fired-up Army

Before the Battle of Arbela in 331 B.C., Darius, the King of Persia, believed he could intimidate Alexander the Great, who with his Greek army had invaded Persia, by sending him a bag of sesame seeds to indicate the great size of his defending troops. Alexander, no dummy, sent back a like-sized bag of mustard seeds to Darius—implying not only the equality of numbers, but the ferociousness of his regiments as well. Whether it was through strength, wiliness, or a stunning public-relations ploy—who knows?—Alexander won, eventually annexing Persia to his empire.

Metered Mustard

Sydney Smith, the English journalist, clergyman, and greens-eater, put his recipe for a favorite salad with mustard, into verse in the eighteenth century:

To make this condiment, your poet begs
The pounded yellow of two hard-boil'd eggs;
Two boil'd potatoes, pass'd through kitchen sieve,
Smoothness and softness to the salad give.
Let onion atoms lurk within the bowl,
And, half suspected, animate the whole.
Of mordant mustard add a single spoon,
Distrust the condiment that bites too soon;
But deem it not, thou man of herbs, a fault,
To add a double quantity of salt;
Four times the spoon with oil of Lucca crown,
And twice with vinegar procured from town;
And lastly, o'er the flavored compound toss
A magic soupçon of anchovy sauce.
Oh, green and glorious! Oh, herbaceous treat!
'Twould tempt the dying anchorite to eat:
Back to the world he'd turn his fleeting soul,

And plunge his fingers in the salad bowl!
Serenely full, the epicure would say,
Fate cannot harm me, I have dined today.

MUSTARD FIRES UP
FOOD OF INDIA

Never go to India, especially Bengal, North India, or
Pakistan, without expecting to eat a lot of mustard in one
form or another. You won't always know it's there, but it
often is.

Mustard seeds are known as *rai* in India and are of the
Brassica juncea species or the oriental strain of brown mustard seeds. To be truly authentic when cooking Indian
cuisine, stick to brown (not black) seeds. If you have to,
move up to *nigra* rather than down to *alba* when *juncea* is
unavailable. Otherwise the nutty mustard flavor you're
looking for will be lacking.

If the brown mustard seeds are not crushed and added,
many Indian recipes call for them to be popped in sizzling
oil before other ingredients are added to the pot. Be careful
to cover the pan immediately after putting in the seeds.
They tend to jump when tossed into hot oil and can cause a
nasty burn—or mess.

Mustard Oil Makes It

As a substitute for *ghee* (clarified butter, the cooking
medium in many Indian recipes), mustard oil is apt to be
used. This is a deep golden, slightly pungent oil pressed
from several kinds of mustard seeds, including field mustard
(*Brassica campestris*), and from rape (*Brassica napus*), and
another member of the family, the turnip (*Brassica rapa*).

Mustard oil is a polyunsaturated oil with a distinctive
flavor and odor when used in cooking. If it is heated to the
smoking point it is not at all pungent because its essential

oils evaporate. If a recipe calls specifically for mustard oil, don't use a substitute because the flavor won't be authentic. Mustard oil is available in food stores specializing in Indian and Oriental products.

For Western recipes the oil can add a subtle mustard flavor. Use it to dress salads, mixed half-and-half with olive or vegetable oil. Use it straight for deep-fat frying or sautéing. Mustard oil is relatively inexpensive and has a unique taste. It adds immeasurably to the flavor of the batter-fried shrimp recipe on page 91.

Mostarda Di Frutta

Although the Italians use little mustard in their cooking, they do find a use for mustard oil in *Mostarda* a specialty of the city of Cremona. *Mostarda* is not mustard but a combination of preserved fruits—figs, plums, grapes, cherries, pumpkin, pears, apricots, and melons—in a sweet syrup containing mustard oil and garlic. Apparently it can be made successfully nowhere else but Cremona, the Lombard city where Stradivarius, Amati, and Guarnieri violins were made. *Mostarda di Frutta* sounds as if it might be a peculiar combination, but actually is no more so than chutney. It is usually served with *bollito misto,* mixed boiled meats, with eel, and with *zampone,* the sausage from Modena. It has the same effect as serving applesauce with pork, mint jelly with lamb, and cranberry sauce with turkey.

Mostarda can be found in this country imported in jars, but it has none of the piquancy of the *Mostarda* one can taste in Italy. The fruits in *Mostarda di Cremona* have a translucent beauty and the captivating look of jewels suspended in a golden syrup.

WHY IT'S CALLED MUSTARD

There is a minor controversy among historians as to how mustard got its name. The Greeks and Romans called the seed *sinapis.* So it is not from the seed that the name derives. The Romans, however, mixed the pounded seeds with grape must (the freshly pressed juice of the fruit before fermentation takes place) and called the result, in Latin, *mustum ardens,* or burning wine. It is likely that our word mustard stems from a contraction of the Latin words, just as the French *moutarde* comes from their word for must, *mout,* and a form of the adjective, *ardent*—burning, hot, fiery.

There is another theory about the word's etymology. It seems that in 1382 Philip the Bold, Duke of Burgundy, marched against Ghent, a city which had broken from his rule. Dijon supplied Philip with a thousand armed men to wage his military campaign. He subdued Ghent and out of gratitude granted the Dijonnais the privilege of using his coat of arms with his motto, *Moulte me tarde,* "I ardently desire." This was carved on the main gate into the city, but an accident destroyed the middle word, leaving only *moult tarde*—burn much. This amused everyone because the merchants of Dijon traded in mustard seed and the seed was given the derisive nickname *moutarde.* This theory is a little farfetched—but far more romantic than "burning wine."

THE SPICE OF LOVE

Mustard is an aphrodisiac. Or so the ancients thought. The Chinese did too. During the Dark Ages it was said to titillate and titivate the senses and was revered as a love spice used in certain teas to increase virility.

Frederick the Great believed in mustard's ability to enhance his masculinity. He combined *powdered mustard with coffee AND champagne* for a drink to have before having his way.

Rabelais wrote that his friars, to increase their lustiness, "began their meal with cheese, ending it with mustard and lettuce, as Martial tells us the ancients did. As each received a dishful of mustard after dinner, they made good the old proverb: *Mustard after dinner/ Is good for saint and sinner.*"

John Davenport, in his book *Aphrodisiacs and Love Stimulants*, privately printed in London in 1877, reported that two physicians, Gesner and Chappel, cured a case of impotence that had lasted for three or four years by repeated immersions of the offending member in a strong infusion of mustard seeds. A distressing problem, yes, but an even more distressing solution.

Mustard was known to the Greeks as an anti-aphrodisiac. Even though one appetite cannot be satisfied by another, sexual desire in men was supposed to be diminished by drinking a decoction of mustard. In fact its ingestion in a fluid state was said to prevent an erection. Had the Greeks been right, civilization would seem to have died out with the Romans, who consumed prodigious amounts of mustard.

Pliny the Elder, the renowned Roman naturalist, insisted, contrary to Greek belief, that mustard overcame lassitude in women. He makes no comment on its effects on men.

MUSTARD IN THE MEDICINE CHEST

Pliny also recommended mustard as a remedy for the bites of most poisonous serpents. Just apply it to the wound, he suggested. If taken internally, he went on, one could eat poisonous mushrooms and survive.

The first to recognize mustard's medicinal qualities was Hippocrates. He treated disease by paying attention to the patient's diet and general regimen and prescribed mustard as a digestive, an emetic, a diuretic, and a stimulant.

Maybe Pliny meant to induce vomiting after eating poisoned mushrooms by using a dose of mustard in hot water as an emetic. It works that way, as Hippocrates knew, and has been usefully employed by laymen and doctors for thousands of years when anything poisonous must immediately be ejected from the stomach through the mouth.

The Romans thought mustard added to a man's strength. Pythagoras, the Greek, said it helped him to think, and promoted it as a brain food. Both the Romans and the Greeks recommended its use in summer—to cause sweating, which, through evaporation, cools the skin.

In folk medicine it has always been a home remedy for a variety of ailments. Early American herb books suggested a foot bath; one said to "lay it on the feet, mixed with other things, in dangerous fevers." The theory was that mustard would cause the blood to rush to the extremities and away from the head, thus reducing the temperature of the upper torso. Reducing the abnormal action of one part of the body by exciting another, suddenly, is why a foot bath was also used to help heal a sluggish liver and headache—also to "sweat out a cold. In the latter case the patient should go straight to bed, sleeping between blankets."

By the eighteenth and nineteenth centuries some physicians relied on mustard foot baths to relieve the symptoms of high blood pressure.

For bronchitis early books advised the application of a mustard plaster. Mustard plasters are still used to relieve coughs and congestion. Simple recipe: Powder a warm, wet dish towel with mustard flour. Apply to chest, powdered side to skin. When skin starts to tingle, leave for ten to fifteen minutes and remove. If skin is sensitive, coat plaster with raw egg white before applying.

The Compleat Vermin Killer and Useful Pocket Companion, published in Dublin in 1778, prescribes: "For violent coughs arising from asthma: Infuse three drachms of garlick and ½ ounce mustard seed in a quart of white wine, let it stand a week and drink it as often as you wish." And when the attack is over, you can always pour what's left on a salad.

Chewing the seeds several times a day when a cold was coming on was said to expel the cold and the attendant mucus. Herbals also promoted mustard as an antiseptic, a breath purifier, and a laxative.

During the Revolutionary War period, wild greens, especially those of the mustard plant, were eagerly hunted, a recent U.S. Department of Agriculture bulletin contends, "as a spring tonic which would cleanse the blood. These greens were an excellent source of Vitamins A and C." They still are.

When the English winters were especially bitter, those who worked out of doors were urged by Mary Thorne Quelch in her *Herbs For Daily Use* to start the day with a cup of hot coffee into which a half teaspoon of "made mustard" had been stirred. The mustard apparently "gives a 'tang' to the coffee yet is not to be tasted otherwise. Milk and sugar should be added as usual. A warming, wonderful glow" is the result.

Mustard is recommended today as a way of adding appeal to salt-free diets. Use the dry powder to make your own, use it straight from the can to season cooked dishes, or look for salt-free Dijons. For weight-loss diets you might be interested to know that most Dijon mustards have only five calories per teaspoon.

Hot Mustard and the Common Cold

As to mustard's curative or restorative powers, all we can report is that since testing the recipes in this book—and eating about sixty pounds of mustard in the process—no one in our family has had a cold. Not even a sniffle. Take that for what it's worth. After all, this was a culinary project, not a medical one.

MUSTARD: ALL YOU'LL
EVER NEED TO KNOW

As is obvious from the preceeding pages, mustard has been celebrated in song and legend throughout the centuries. Interestingly, though, almost all contemporary information comes from a single source—an article by Alexandre Dumas that is in reality an advertisement for the House of Alexandre Bornibus, a nineteenth-century Parisian mustard manufacturer. The ad appeared preceded and followed by its illustrious copywriter's name in his own *Grand Dictionnaire de Cuisine*, published in Paris in 1873. It is of interest for its historical and botanical content. It's also amusing because it is so long-winded and makes the merest mention of Bornibus mustard, along with Dumas's endorsement, only at the very end. Our present-day promotional sophisticates on Madison Avenue would never approve.

Whether Dumas did his homework or, being a storyteller by trade, embellished some of the material, the information contained in the article has become accepted as fact by the culinary establishment. This much-quoted piece is reproduced in its entirety for your enjoyment.

Grand Dictionnaire

de

Cuisine

par

Alexandre Dumas

Paris

Alphonse Lemerse, Editeur

Passage Choiseul 27 – 29

Paris 1873

Answer to an anonymous letter addressed to gluttons of all countries.

I sometimes get strange letters; here is one that I received this morning:

Sir:
   You are, they say, at the same time a great literary figure and an excellent cook.
   You have occupied yourself, like Lucrece, with the origin of men and of things.
   Could you do me the enormous favor to tell me, chronologically, to what epoch mustard goes back?
   Etymologically, where its name comes from?
   Botanically, to what family the plant belongs?
   Culinarily, which preparations you prefer?
   I would be immensely grateful if you could render me that service.

If my anonymous correspondent, instead of requesting a public answer, had told me where to answer him directly—or by post office box—under a fictitious name—even under an initial—I would not be telling you this story which has, I must admit, no other reason for being told.

I am so totally convinced, like Pic de la Mirandole, by the fact that one can speak with charm about all known facts, that I immediately adhere to your desires, without being too afraid that my readers will complain about it.

We are going to frankly get to the heart of the matter.

You ask me, dear anonymous, to what epoch mustard goes back.

Permit me to busy myself with the egg before the chicken, and with the seed before the plant.

The Greeks and the Romans did not know prepared mustard in pots, as we sell it today. They knew it as a seed, and used that seed in stews, and in powder form for roasts, just as we use our mustard nowadays.

Greeks and Romans used the same word to designate it,

which would seem to prove that this condiment passed from Greece to Italy, from Athens to Rome.

They used the word sinapis both for the seed or the flour of mustard. Medicine adopted that name.

Aristophanes and Menandre in their satirical pieces preserved the recipes of several stews in which mustard was an ingredient.

Both the Old and the New Testament often refer to "seeds of sênevé," the French translation of the hebrew word mustard.

In the somber imprecations of the prophets against the kingdoms of Juda and Israel, the seeds of sênevé played a prominent part as a metaphor.

The early Romans used it in its natural state and in powder form in their meals; but the Romans by the end of the Republic and Empire had too corrupt a taste to use it in that primitive simplicity. They combined it with brine of tuna and made a sauce called "muria."

Then they used a tenth or twelfth part mustard for their horrible concoction called "garum" which consisted of the intestines, head and gills of anchovies, and the same ingredients from mackerel and sea-bream. They crushed the mess with mushrooms, laurel, thyme and then added, what? Nobody knows. Perhaps nothing.

There would be the wit of the joke; and one sold that horrible mixture for 500 francs for 1½ liters.

Since the Romans had a highly developed taste for pork, the use of sinapis was very important to them.

Plautus, who lived 240 years before Jesus Christ and who was a contemporary of Ennius, Scipio the African, Syphax, Massinissa and Hannibal, seems to have hated mustard as much as Horace hated garlic. His chef in Pseudolus, called mustard a horrible poison, which can't be pounded or ground without causing eyes to tear and in Truculentus, on the same subject, he has Astrophius state that "If this man would nourish himself with mustard he could not be more sullen or more of a lunatic."

Pliny the Elder who suffocated in the ashes that buried Pompeii during the eruption of Vesuvius advised to use mustard as a seasoning combined with vinegar.

But wait, here goes Columella who in his book De re rustica, written in 42 A.D. gives us pretty closely the recipe for modern mustard:

> Clean with great care seeds of sênevé; sift it, then wash it with cold water and then when it is washed, let it soak in cold water for 2 hours; reactivate it and after squeezing it by hand, put it in a new, or very clean, mortar and crush it under a pestle. When this is well crushed, move the paste to the center of the mortar and flatten it by hand; after having it thus compressed, make some furrows, in which you scatter hot coals with water and saltpeter poured over these. This will remove all bitterness from this seed and will keep it from molding. Remove it from the mortar so that the moisture disappears completely. On this mustard pour strong white vinegar, mix it thoroughly with the pestle and pass it through a sieve.

You see, here we are in 42 A.D. and if it weren't for the advice of the celebrated gastronomist Courchamps, who, without absolutely forbidding vinegar, prefers hot water or white wine added to it, we are devilishly close to our modern mustard.

Would you like it slightly more perfected? Here is a recipe which dates from the 4th century. It comes from Palladius, son of Exuperantius, prefect of the Greeks:

> Reduce to a powder a pint-and-a-half of mustard seed; add a pound of honey, a pound of Spanish oil, a pint of strong white vinegar, crush together and use.

You have now seen sinapis pass from Greece to Italy and now you see sênevé pass from Rome into Gaul.

But the Barbarians overran Europe, and all the uncultured

---

peoples which came from India, Tibet, and elsewhere, did not know mustard, the refinement of two cultures, and so removed it from the culinary repertory of the vanquished.

Charlemagne, who chased the Norman pirates away, Charlemagne, that magnificent emperor who in his heyday had his table served by kings, the kings' table served by dukes, the dukes' table by marquises, the marquises' table by counts, the counts' by barons, the barons' by knights, the knights' by grooms so that if the kings breakfasted at 9 A.M., the grooms breakfasted at 9 P.M.

Charlemagne, in his Capitularies, speaks of sénevé as an edible plant whose leaves one ate either cooked or in salads. But of crushed mustard seed diluted in vinegar or wine there is no mention. Not a word.

Dijon, alone preserved the first recipe of Palladius and therefore, if it was not the inventor, it was at least the restorer of mustard.

When did the honor of restoring this indispensible condiment to the Table come to the "Dijonnais"?

It is impossible to know. All that we know is that Etienne Boileau, prefect of Paris under St. Louis, authorized the vinegar makers to make mustard.

In the "Cries of Paris" of the 13th century we find:

"Vinegar is beautiful! Good mustard vinegar!"

At that time, the sauce makers, at the dinner hour, brought sauces to the houses and ran around the streets of Paris crying: "Mustard sauce! Garlic sauce! Scallion sauce! Vinegar sauce! Ravigote sauce!"

Anyone who didn't want to eat dry meat opened his window and called for the sauce vendor.

He would then immediately be served with the sauce of his choice.

One understands that imitators used the Dijon name and exploited it, but Dijon kept its supremacy nonetheless.

In the "Sayings of the Aportoile," a 13th-century manuscript, one finds mention of Moutarde de Dijon.

In the proverbs of Jean Millot, of the 14th century, one reads:

> There is no town, if not Dijon.
> There is no mustard but in Dijon.

It was useless for the South to make mustard and substitute wine for vinegar. A new slogan established the tenacious superiority of the Burgundian capital: "The mustard of St. Maxence is good but the one from Dijon is better."

During the celebrations at Rouvres in 1336, given by the Burgundian Duke Eudes IV for King Philippe of Valois, 3 hectolitres of mustard were consumed at one dinner.

At 9 A.M. and at 6 P.M., one would find children all over Paris buying mustard for a farthing. When asked what time it was, the reply was: "The time children go out to get mustard."

It wasn't only the King of France, Philippe of Valois, who ate his meat with mustard; the kings of England did the same.

According to Froissart when Edward III invaded France in 1453, he ordered his captains to burn everything along their way. The magistrates of Saint-Didier begged him not to burn the plains since, said they, all the victuals will be burned and the result will be great famine.

"Bah, bah," answered the ferocious Plantagenet, "war without fire is like blood sausage without mustard."

The first cookbook to appear in France *The Viandier* by Taillevent under King Charles VII, gave great praise to mustard.

Here is what he says in a rather difficult French which we will try to make readable to all:

One evening, after a great battle against the English, King Charles VII and his inseparable companions, Dunois, Lattire, and Xaintrailles, looked for lodging in the small town of St. Menehould in which were left standing only 5 or 6 houses, the town having been burned.

King Charles VII and his followers were starving. The

ruined and ravaged country lacked everything. Finally, they were able to find four pigs' feet and three chickens. Since the King had neither cook nor chef with him, they asked the wife of a poor toolmaker to cook the chickens. The pigs' feet just had to be put on the grill. The good woman roasted the chickens, dipped them in egg batter, rolled them in seasoned bread crumbs, and then basted them with a mustard sauce. She then served these to the King and his companions who devoured everything leaving only the chicken bones.

King Charles VII, who ate very well, afterwards asked for *chickens à la Ste. Menehould* very often. Taillevent, who knew what he wanted, served to him chickens prepared in the same manner as the ones prepared by the wife of the poor toolmaker.

Louis XI who liked to appear for dinner unexpectedly at the homes of his good friends, the Parisian bourgeoisie, almost always carried his personal mustard pot with him.

The "stories" of J. Riboteau, general comptroller of Burgundy, tell us that in 1477 an order was placed by him with an apothecary of Dijon for 20 lbs of mustard for the personal use of the King.

Finally, and to finish by a little-known anecdote, I think we will tell you that of the popes who held such magnificent court at Avignon, Pope John XXII was one of the ones that loved the pleasures of the table. He adored mustard, put it in everything and not knowing what to do with a ne'er-do-well-nephew, gave him the title of "First Mustardmaker."

From there comes the expression that a vain fool believes himself to be the First Mustardmaker of the Pope.

On their return to Rome, the Popes brought their love of mustard with them. Leo X and Clarence VII of the Medicis were great lovers of the spice. However the mustard that they were served and which was the one being used at the time had really no great similarity with ours of today.

It was made of scraps of stale bread, almonds, crushed

mustard seed soaked in water with vinegar, then passed through a sieve.

Tell us now that it is a waste of time to read this. We have already given our readers at least two almost-unknown recipes!

I thought I should limit my mustard study to the letter received yesterday. However, thinking seriously of the honorable rank that mustard holds in our modern culinary repertory—like a gold key of appetite—I am forced to give additional information. Material and facts abound and I doubt if there is any condiment that recommends itself to the degustation of gourmets more.

Mustard even has its coat of arms, accorded by Louis XIV, blue with a silver funnel.

Up to that time, the beginnings of the 17th century, Dijon only made dry mustard, in cakes or lozenges. Jean Hiebault is the first author to offer a recipe equivalent to the one that we use today, namely mustard seed crushed and watered down with strong vinegar.

Here is a more complicated recipe which can be found in the "Messages Parisien"; it is pretty much what we have today:

If you want to make a good mustard without much trouble, it is said to allow the mustard to soak overnight in good vinegar, then crush it very well with a mill, and then little by little dilute the vinegar. And, if you have leftover spices, jelly, claret and sauces, crush all of these together and let it stand and form the mustard.

Oddly enough, mustard had a resurgence with the discovery of the Cape of Good Hope and America. Christopher Columbus brought to Europe West Indian Spices, while Vasco de Gama brought in the ones from the East Indies.

Spices were very influential on the "cuisine" of the 16th, 17th, and even the 18th century, mostly the slightly perfumed spices such as vanilla, nutmeg, and clove which were already well-known in France but so expensive that they were only given as presents to, for instance, the judge who renders a decision in your behalf or to the lawyer who pleads your case. These spices became more commonplace when Antonio de Abreu and Francisco Serrao discovered the Spice Islands in 1511. In either 1607 or 1608 the Dutch won them from the Portuguese and these modern Phoenicians understood the enormous value of their conquest and decided to make the spice trade a Dutch monopoly.

Therefore they concluded a treaty with the sultan of Ternate, their vassal, and other sovereigns of these small islands allowing the spice trees to be transferred to Amboine and Banda and otherwise uprooted.

As indemnity for the loss of this particular trade they paid them an annuity of 70,000 francs.

The sale was so important that they did not hesitate to build three forts to stop any smuggling: the forts were Holland, Orange, and Wilhelmstadt.

Besides these three main forts, nine more were built on different parts of the islands.

A fleet of twenty ships, put at the disposal of the governor of Amboine, patrolled the islands constantly.

Let's go back to our subject, from which spices removed us, and which Rabelais, great expert in the gourmet art (as he himself admits), calls a natural remedy and a restorer of the digestive tract.

Mustard, left on the sidelines by this eruption of eastern and western spices fought bravely.

Dijon, the great mustard production center, felt that their product needed a charter to completely reassure the public about methods and ingredients used in its manufacture.

Therefore, the mustard makers and the vinegar makers of Dijon received, in 1634, charters which joined them to the other crafts of the town and entitled them alone to the fabrication of mustard.

The fourteenth article of the rule stated:

The apprentices and the companions making mustard and selling and retailing it through the city, will have to be healthy and their linens and their clothes will have to be neat and modest under pain of ten cents fine.

On top of that, article twenty allowed them only one retail store in town so that they couldn't deny from whence it came.

Finally, under pain of another 10 cents fine, they had to have a trademark on their barrels.

They could not rely anymore on the procession of children, who sent out to buy mustard twice a day, and instead sent their young apprentices out to hawk their particular mustard.

The young mustard makers, fearing neither God nor devil, went to Christian gatherings and churches calling out about their mustard, interrupting even the most sacred moments and thereafter were forbidden to enter the churches under the pain of prison. They were also forced to stay home on Sundays.

Twenty-three vinegar-mustard makers of Dijon adhered to the rules. In the middle of their signatures one recognizes the name of Naigeon.

Not withstanding all this, the popularity of mustard decreased. It was felt that in acidity and variety it left something to be desired. At that time, Jean Naigeon, great-grandson of the one who signed the rules of the twenty-three vinegar makers, had an inspiration. He changed one substance in the production of mustard which brought on a resurgence of sales and a revival of favor.

It was a stroke of genius.

Jean Naigeon was the first to substitute verjuice for vinegar. This is the juice extracted from grapes before their maturity. Consequently, no more sugar, no more acetic acid, but only tartaric, citric and malic acids.

Jean Naigeon, was the father of the other Naigeon, librarian at the Arsenal, atheist and friend of Holbach, who published an edition of Diderot's works.

Grimod de la Reynière, illustrious gastronome, author of

the *Dictionary of the Gluttons,* could not stand Naigeon and labeled him an atheist.

The opinion of this illustrious gastronomist almost dethroned Dijon mustard after a reign of five centuries. His culinary opinions were archaic. Grandson of a pork butcher, his father had bought a title and kept a coat of arms: blue and gold with a natural pig's foot, and on the blue a silver ham.

During the youth of Grimod de la Reynière, a great revolution in mustard began.

Paris was beginning to become a serious competitor to Dijon.

The revolution started in 1742.

A Parisian vinegar maker named Capitaine, started to use white vinegar instead of red and added to his fine mustard, capers and anchovy paste.

These innovations were very favorably received.

Ten years later another vinegar maker named Maille made himself a European reputation in his speciality.

Named Privileged Supplier to Mme de Pompadour, he took as well the title of Vinegar Distiller to the King of France and the Emperors of Germany and Russia. An intelligent man who understood the sensuality of the time, he started by making vinegar for the use of men and women; his clientele soon consisted of all the elegants, the petty aristocrats, duchesses, marquises, countesses, young coxcombs and gallant bishops; working through the boudoir was a sure path to the kitchen.

Before Maille there were only 9 species of vinegar. He added 92 clean and healthy ones. He also increased the flavorings of table vinegars. His mustards numbered eighty-four. Red mustard, fine mustard with capers, fine mustard with anchovies, powdered mustard, garlic mustard, tarragon mustard, nasturtium mustard, lemon mustard, à la Choiseul, à la Choisy, in cans, fines herbes, Grecian, à la Marechals, à la Marquise, à la Queen, Roman, with truffles. All were his inventions except for mustard with capers and with anchovies.

The most popular ones were ravigote, garlic, truffles, anchovies, and tarragon.

Maille's mustard is still being used and is even the preferred mustard of certain knowledgeable gourmets.

At the time of Maille, Bordin at the same time in 1726, invented a health mustard, mustard with champagne, with mushrooms, rose mustard, Italian style, with vanilla, and with Spanish garlic.

In 1812, counting the twenty-nine kinds of new mustards invented by Acloque, pupil and successor of Maille, France possessed without counting the Capitaine and Dijon mustards, eighty-four species of mustard. Grimod de la Reynière then called attention to three new mustards, which brought the number up to ninety-three. *(Editor's Note: Dumas was noted as a writer, not a mathematician.)*

Those three mustards were from Châlons-sur-Saône, Besançon, and Saint-Brieuc.

This is what this illustrious taster, who seemed to have a marked preference for Mssrs. Maille and Bordin (who I suspect were constant and lucrative subscribers of the *Almanach des Gourmands*) states:

> An apothecary, from Saint-Brieuc, has just opened a mustard factory which is not without merit and which produces mostly a mustard with lots of strength and good kick. It is already making inroads in Ancient Armorique and the Cotentin.
>
> Mr. Maout, which is what one calls this manufacturer, and whose name, as you can see, is made up of the first five letters in mustard, plans to open an establishment in Paris.

Even just this little that was said about the product of Mr. Maout made people aware of him. Drs. Gastald, Portalis, and Cambacérès declared for Maout's mustard and as long as France was involved in dining with a certain delicacy, celtic mustard appeared on the best tables along with the mustards of Maille and Bordin.

This triumvirate, luckier than the one of Octave and Lepide, reigned for more than half a century on French tables.

The chronology of mustard establishes the route of its geneological tree starting in Greece, Judea, Italy, and reading into the second part of the nineteenth century. I will answer the final three questions of our anonymous writer briefly in a few pages.

Let's go on to question two. Etymologically, where does mustard come from?

On this there are controversies as with most etymologies. The people from Dijon who profess to have invented but who really only were the promulgators lean on the following fact. From this fact, they derive the name of the precious condiment which is our subject.

In 1381, Philippe le Hardi, Duke of Burgundy, marched against Ghent in revolt against his nephew Charles VI. The mayor of Dijon, Jehan Poissonnet, enriched by the sales of mustard, furnished the Duke with 10,000 armed men fully paid for by the city. Upon returning from this successful expedition, the Duke gave the people many privileges such as owning lands and also the right to wear his coat of arms and his motto: *Moult me tarde*.

Pots and barrels of mustard were shipped from Jehan Poissonnet's factory with the arms and motto of the Duke. The Dijonnais maintain that the word mustard is an abbreviation of, as well as a conjunction of, Philippe le Hardi's motto: *Moult me tarde*.

Let's say in passing that Philippe le Hardi was the sublime child that defended to the end his father, King Jean, at the battle of Poitiers. On the evening of the battle, he slapped an Englishman for not kneeling in front of the royal prisoner when handing him the washbasin.

What is most probable is that the word comes from the

Latin *mustum ardens,* which means burning must, from which one made mustard.

This is what the great Boerhaave, who lived in the 17th and 18th centuries says:

In Italia cum musto sinapis conterebatur,
unde dixerunt *mustum ardens,* hinc mustardum.

Which in English means:

In Italy the seed of black sênevé was crushed with the must, this was then called *mout ardent,* moutarde.

This then, if our anonymous correspondent will find it acceptable, is where the word mustard comes from etymologically.

Now let's try to tell him what plant family it belongs to.

Botanically, mustard belongs to siliceous tetradynamy, family of crucifers. Julia de Fonteuille counts twenty families; other botanists count as many as forty. This plant is biannually herbaceous. The leaves vary a lot but most of the time are tapped and serrated.

The fruit is a bivalve silique and the seeds are globular.

As we have said, there are great quantities of different mustards. Only three are used by doctors and mustard makers.

Black mustard (sinapis nigra)
Wild or field mustard (sinapis arvensis)
and White mustard (sinapis alba).

It is this last one which was introduced in England in the middle of the eighteenth century and was recommended by the doctors Trousseau and Pidoux, and of which modern charlatanism tried to make into the universal panacea.

It is so fertile that according to Fuscher de Gresheim, from a pound that he sowed in a field of ninety perches, he harvested five hundred fifty-eight pounds.

Here is the name in various languages. In Greek and Latin, we have already said *sinapis;* in English, *mustard;* in German, *mustersenft;* in Spanish, *mostazza;* in Italian, *mostarda;* in Russian, *gortscheza;* in Arabic *kherdal;* and in Hindustani, *rai.*

The word *moutards,* which is childrens' slang, came from the habit which we spoke of before, of sending children out for mustard in the fourteenth and fifteenth centuries.

Culinarily, you ask me which of the mustards I prefer.

Until I tasted and appreciated the mustard of Alexandre Bornibus, I preferred the aromatic mustards of Maille and Bordin to all the others. But when chance brought that one to me, I felt that this was the one that one day would reign supreme.

I say chance, for this is the way it happened:

I was writing a novel in which the most important action took place in Bourg-en-Bresse. Looking for the shortest way to get there, I was told to go to Mâcon and there take the branch line to Bourg.

I arrived very sleepy in Dijon. I heard the cry: Dijon, Dijon! and in my sleepy state, confusion reigned. Was it Dijon, or was it Mâcon with the side road to Bourg? I could not remember.

Since I only had one suitcase with me, I jumped out of my compartment and ran out and asked for the branch line to Bourg. The ticket taker, who did not know what I meant, did not answer me. I therefore, kept on going into the courtyard. In the courtyard I found a coachman and asked him for the line to Bourg. To which Bourg? To Bourg-en-Bresse. Oh, for that you have to go to Mâcon.

I tried to get back into my compartment. The attendant asked for my ticket.

"My ticket? I gave it to you earlier. Look at the tickets you received and you will find one to Mâcon."

As he looked, the locomotive coughed, spit, sneezed, and took off.

Well, said the attendant laughing, you'll be the first one here for tomorrow's train.

But, said I, for me to take off tomorrow, you will have to give my ticket back.

Here it is, he said, and yes, it is for Mâcon. Well, stay here.

OK, I said, I will take this advantage to see the cathedral and then visit my poor friend, Louis Boulanger.

Louis Boulanger, a painter whose first canvasses showed the most promise, was a director of the Dijon Museum, and I was very excited at this opportunity to see him again.

However, I could not arrive there at eleven P.M. Instead, I went to the Hotel du Parc and requested supper.

I was served two lamb chops and half a cold chicken.

What mustard do you want? asked the waiter.

Dijon mustard, of course.

I know, said he, sounding as though he thought me a complete imbecile, but do you want men's or ladies' mustard?

Oh, oh, said I, and what difference is there between men's and women's mustard?

Ladies' mustard.

OK, ladies' mustard.

Well, sir, since ladies' palates are more delicate than men's, the ordinary Dijon mustard is too strong and spicy for them, so Mr. Bornibus invented a special mustard.

Who is Mr. Bornibus?

Well, sir, he is a great and fashionable Parisian mustard maker.

Here, the talk is only of *his* mustard.

It is true that I knew his reputation, but so far, I didn't know his mustard. It would be funny if I tasted it in Dijon. Give me some.

Which one of the two?

Both of them.

You are going to eat ladies' mustard?

If I can eat the strong, I can eat the weak.

And the waiter served me two kinds of mustard with my chops.

I am not a great devotee of mustard. Being endowed with

an excellent stomach, I have never made great use of this *preface to appetite,* as Grimond de la Reynière calls it; but I must say that this time, at the sight of the beautiful canary yellow color of this admirable apéritif, I plunged my wooden spoon into the mustard pot and made two pyramids on my plate, one of men's mustard, the other of ladies' mustard.

Since you ask my advice, sir, I must say that from there on in, I stripped the poor man of all his mustard, and rallied myself around Bornibus mustard.

Upon my return to Paris, I visited Mr. Bornibus's studio, 60 Boulevard de la Villette. He willingly showed me his establishment and explained that his products obtained their superiority because of the perfection of his tools which were of his invention, and mostly because of the combination and the choice of his raw materials.

This, I think, my dear anonymous correspondent, is all you desire from me, chronologically, etymologically, botanically, and culinarily.

MUSTARDS: HOW TO CHOOSE THEM

Not all mustard brands, especially the imported varieties, are distributed nationally. However, many of those listed here should be available in your area. We suggest you scout department-store gourmet sections for the more esoteric brands. Most American mustards have universal distribution, and Grey Poupon, made in California, is an admirable substitute for imported Dijons, though not quite as strong.

Imported Dijons vary in taste—some are hotter than others, some saltier, some contain spices. Conduct your own taste test. Discover which ones suit your palate best for cooking and table use. Try the flavored Dijons too. As mustards increase in popularity, manufacturers are adding more and more flavored mustards to their lines. At a recent food fair in Germany, a mustard appeared flecked with truffles. This kind of lily-gilding, especially at a projected retail price of $25 for a 3½ oz. jar, is taking the craze for flavored mustard too far.

When purchasing this condiment, don't buy a jar whose contents have darkened on top, don't buy more than you can use up in a reasonable length of time (or it will lose its pizzazz), and do store opened jars in the refrigerator.

French's—the standard hot-dog condiment, heavy on vinegar and turmeric

Gulden's Spicy Brown—a delicatessen mustard, for cold cuts and franks

Gulden's Diablo—a spicier version of the brown, but not hot, in spite of its name

Gulden's Creamy Mild—as yellow as French's

Kosciusko—a robust delicatessen mustard

Mister Mustard—supposed to be hot but it's not; delicatessen mustard

Beaver American—tangy sandwich spread, good with cheese, hamburgers

Nances—the hottest American prepared mustard, on the sweet side

Cornwall Farms Honey Mustard—sweet mustard in a large clay crock, made in Connecticut

Greylore Farms—nice, strong aroma but tastes mild and sweet

A. Baurer's Dusseldorf—an everyday delicatessen mustard made in U.S.A.

CREOLE MUSTARD

The background is French/Spanish, weighted on the French side.

Zatarain's—from New Orleans, an appealing flavor, but no heat

Reese—not hot

Only those marked "English" are the fiery kind kindled with water; the others are English packers' versions of French and other styles.

Colman's English—hot, smooth, authentic

Colman's Dijon—an okay try at the real thing

Colman's Meaux—coarse-textured French style

Colman's German—mild, dark, herbal flavor

Colman's French—dark-brown Bordeaux style

Colman's American—why import what we have?

Colman's Cream Salad—very mild, very pale

Crabtree & Evelyn's Mild Honey—a grainy, sweetish mustard

Crabtree & Evelyn's Black Mustard—grainy, made with dark-brown seeds, quite pungent

Crabtree & Evelyn's Especially Robust—grainy, laced with chilies, peppers, quite hot

Crabtree & Evelyn's Tarragon—grainy, with lashings of the herb

Gordon's English Vineyard—grainy texture with crunch

Gordon's English Farmhouse—hot, with hulls included

Gordon's English Green Peppercorn—a grainy green peppercorn mustard, on the hot side

Invemore—made with Scotch whiskey and herbs from the highlands

Elsenham—a hot English mustard with hulls included

Military Mustard—made in Wales with chili vinegar, chilis, *and* cayenne; searing!

ENGLISH AND AMERICAN POWDERED MUSTARDS

From England:

  Colman's Genuine Double Superfine—very hot

  Colman's Double Superfine—medium hot, still strong

  Colman's Special Mild Blend—less hot than medium

From the U.S.:

  Durkee's Powdered Mustard—not hot at all

CONTINENTAL MUSTARDS

Savora—savory, sweet, with pickled onion juice added

Gourmet Award—Viennese style out of St. Paul, Minnesota, made with imported Moselle wine

CHINESE PREPARED MUSTARDS

Dynasty Brand—hot, salty, perfumy, not the familiar Chinese-restaurant taste

Beaver Chinese—extra hot, closer to the restaurant stuff

Trader Vic's Chinese Mustard Powder—hot, to mix yourself

ISRAELI MUSTARD

Telma—somewhere between Dijon and Rochester—gastronomically, not geographically

RUSSIAN MUSTARDS

Beaver Russian—American made, sweet and hot

Sable & Rosenfeld Russian—made in Canada, sweet, hot elegantly flavored

GERMAN MUSTARDS

Hengstenberg Delicatess Senf—Dusseldorf Style, close to Dijon, but mild and slightly sweet

Beaver Dusseldorf—smooth, a little hot, flavored with horseradish

Lion Brand—another Dusseldorf by Frenzl, salty, not to be used as a substitute for Dijon

Enjiansenf—Bavarian style, which means sweet and dark

SWEDISH MUSTARDS

Druvan Gastgivare Senap Hot—chewy, with husks, slightly hot and sweet

Druvan Gastigivare Senap Sweet—smooth, sweet, nice with herrings

Slott's Skansk—sweet, grainy, with the taste of cinnamon

SPECIALTY MUSTARDS AND MUSTARD SAUCES

Bocquet Mustard Sauce—the lazy man's dressing for cold shrimp, chicken, salads; sharp, vinegary

Petite Marmite Mustard Sauce—from the Palm Beach restaurant, a combination of mayo, French mustard, tarragon, vinegar, Worcestershire

"21" Sauce Maison—a mustard base with tomato sauce, spices, Worcestershire, named after the famous N.Y. restaurant

Dondi Mostarda di Cremona—jarred sweet glazed fruits in mustard oil syrup; imported, but so toned-down, it's hardly recognizable

HP Mustard Piccalilli Chow-Chow—chunky, with vegetables; vinegary, sharp, mustardy

The variations of taste from one brand to another are due to the substitution of vinegar for Burgundy wine in some cases, a heavy hand with salt in others, or a difference in amount and combinations of additional spices, but basically they all should have a smooth, clean, sharp taste and some heat (not an overpowering burn like English made-mustard, but an undertone of mustard strength and pungency).

Taste as many as you can find until you discover one that suits you. Stick with it. Your recipes will then have your own personal stamp.

What follows is a descriptive listing of brands.

Amora—concentrated flavor, the French best-seller, excellent for cooking

Benedicta—nutty, smooth, tangy

Bocquet Yvetot—well-rounded flavor, smooth, a trifle salty

Bornibus—the original Dijon competitor from Paris

Bourdier d'Auvergne—called "Fancy City"; smooth, strong

Crabtree & Evelyn—English name, French-made flavor

Dessaux Fils—balanced, smooth, rather salty

Devos-Lemmens—should be called "Dijon-style" because it's from Belgium

Fauchon—sharp; metallic aftertaste

Jaret—fine flavor, nicely balanced

La Charcutière—mellow, sharp, salty

Les Frères Troigros—a revered name in haute cuisine does a haute Dijon

Maille—light, slightly salty, excellent cooking mustard

Maître Jacques—quality mustard, a little salty, versatile

Moutarde du Lion—strong and zesty, flavorful

Old Monk—a traditional Dijon

Parizot—fresh, sharp

Paul Courcellet—smooth, aromatic

Pikarome—hot and smooth, not overpowering

Queen's Gate—funny name for a Dijon but worth a try

Reine de Dijon—piquant, salty, pleasant

Roland—not "extra strong," as the label claims

Temeraire—sharp; spicy undertone

FLAVORED MUSTARDS

Most flavored mustards are made with a brand's original Dijon recipe, with herbs or other flavorings added. Use them for the table or use them in recipes where the herb or spice flavoring is an ingredient.

Maille—all are top-notch, good quality, moderately priced
        Tarragon
        Green Peppercorn
        Shallot
        Red Pepper (not chili peppers)
        Lemon

Maître Jacques
        Tarragon (with coarsely chopped fresh leaves)
        Green Peppercorn (you can't see them; hot)
        Hot Red Pepper (pure fire)

Devos-Lemmens
        Moutarde au poivre vert de Madagasgar (the mustard's from Belgium)

Amora—the top brand in France has two top contenders
        Tarragon
        Lemon

Bornibus—the Parisian mustard has two flavors
>Tarragon
>Green Peppercorn

Louit Bocquet
>Green Peppercorn

Crabtree & Evelyn—all are French Dijons with flavors added
>Tarragon
>Green Peppercorn
>Lime
>Provençal Herbs

Pikarome
>Tarragon
>Green Peppercorn

Florida—the mustard in the champagne-bottle jar comes up with an interesting idea, tomato-flavor, but it's not successful (see page 76 for Tomato-Herb Mustard recipe).

Fauchon—the gourmet paradise on the Place de la Madeleine sends us a bouquet of flavored mustards. Caution: some make it; some don't. Taste them before you decide to use them in a recipe.
>Green Peppercorn
>Exotic (mixture of herbs and spices)
>Tarragon
>Garlic-Parsley
>Lemon-Lime
>Orange
>Horseradish
>Tzigane Paprika
>Mint
>Xeres Sherry
>Herbs of Provence
>Black Olive
>Olive & Anchovy

Pink Pepper
Muscatel

Raoul Gey With Lime—lovely flavor for fish and salads

Bocquet With Herbs—the herbs take over here

Bourdier d'Auvergne
 Green Peppercorn City Mustard
 Fresh Tarragon City Mustard

———— CHAMPAGNE MUSTARDS ————

Moutarde Florida—prepared with Champagne District wine in Epernay; refillable champagne-bottle jar

Roland Champagne—a knock-off of the Florida packaging that doesn't taste like mustard

Cherchies Champagne Mustard—from Pennsylvania, a sweet cooked mustard made with champagne vinegar and eggs, very smooth, sweet, and fresh-tasting; a local brand moving fast

Arizona Champagne Mustard Sauce—in regular and hot strengths, good as sandwich spread, dip, or to add to salad dressings

———— GRAINY MUSTARDS ————

These are the old style, *à l'ancienne,* mustards with husks left in. Some are coarser-textured than others; some even contain the whole seed, to enrich texture and taste. Unless you use mustard in large quantities or must have the crock, buy the small jars if you want the flavor to last down to the final spoonful.

Amora Old-Fashioned Mustard—winey, tiny-grained, excellent flavor

Maître Jacques Grained Mustard—salty, flavorful, coarse-grained

Pommery Moutarde de Meaux—the first to be promoted here

Maille Old Style—always reliable

Raoul Gey Burgundy—tart; pleasant texture

Pikarome Old Style—another reliable brand

Les Frères Troigros Country Mustard—chic, pricey

Paul Courcellet Traditional Mustard—coarse-textured

Crabtree & Evelyn Old Fashioned—good flavor and texture

La Charcutière Old Time—small-grained

Bourdier d'Auvergne—whole grain "country mustard"

SALT-FREE DIJONS

Maître Jacques Salt Free—nice flavor even without the salt

Reine Dijon Salt Free—a coup for those previously stuck with tasteless health-food store diet mustards

Crabtree & Evelyn—several flavors

MUSTARD SEEDS

There are several familiar supermarket brands which usually give you only white seeds. Stores specializing in loose spices almost always stock brown and/or black seeds along with white ones.

MUSTARDS: MAKING YOUR OWN

It's simple to make your own mustard as a condiment and for cooking. The mustard recipes which follow are all *very* hot. They will remain hot indefinitely if refrigerated almost immediately.

If you'd rather they be milder, *age* them. After sealing in jars, put them on a shelf in the cupboard and forget about them for two or three weeks or longer. Taste once in a while. When they reach the degree of mildness you like, transfer them to the refrigerator and begin to use them. Refrigeration arrests the aging process.

In some parts of the country, flavored Dijon mustards are unavailable. You can mix your own by starting with a jar of plain Dijon and adding to it fresh or dried herbs and seasonings to taste.

Here are some suggested flavoring agents which can add a little zing to plain Dijon.

Green Peppercorns—drained and slightly crushed
Lemon—the juice and grated rind
Lime—the juice and grated rind
Orange—the juice and grated rind
Fennel—ground seeds
Capers—drained and chopped
Sage—chopped fresh or crumbled dry leaves

Apricot—jam or jelly
Onion—fresh grated
Basil—chopped fresh or crumbled dry leaves
Dill—snipped fresh or crushed dry or ground seeds
Tarragon—chopped fresh or crumbled dry leaves
Oregano—chopped fresh or crumbled dry leaves
Hot Pepper—dried crushed flakes or chopped fresh chilies
Pickle—chopped dill, bread and butter, garlic, or gherkin
Paprika—sweet or hot powder
Mint—chopped fresh or crumbled dry
Garlic—chopped or crushed cloves
Olive—chopped green or black
Parsley—chopped fresh or crumbled dry
Shallot—chopped
Chervil—crumbled dry
Anchovy—paste or drained chopped flat fillets
Dried Mushrooms—soaked, drained, and chopped

Start by mixing in a little at a time, until you achieve the forcefulness of flavor you want. Allow a few hours for the flavors to meld before using. Also try combining some of the seasonings, such as caper and anchovy; olive and garlic; tarragon, basil, and hot pepper; pickle and dill; lemon and lime; anchovy and black olive; and so on.

• Keep an opened jar of mustard sparkling-fresh longer by floating a slice of lemon on the surface. Close jar well and refrigerate.

• When mixing mustard powder to a paste, try using cream sherry to give it a slightly sweet and nutty taste.

• Hot English Mustard •

¼ cup dry mustard
2 tablespoons cold water

Place the dry mustard in a small bowl. Gradually add the water, mixing thoroughly until smooth. Allow the mixture to stand for at least 10 minutes to develop its flavor.

If larger amounts are needed, this recipe may be increased proportionately and made in a blender or processor fitted with steel blade.

For variation, use the same method, substituting for the water other liquids such as vinegar, wine, stale beer, milk, or even flat champagne. If the mustard is too hot for your palate, add one teaspoon of sugar to tone down its bite. A teaspoon of heavy cream added also turns down the flames.

Serve with hot or cold roast beef, lamb, Chinese spareribs, corned beef, and cold cuts.

Makes approximately ¼ cup.

• Horseradish Mustard •

1 cup dry mustard
½ cup granulated sugar
½ teaspoon salt
½ cup tarragon vinegar

¼ cup olive oil
½ teaspoon lemon juice
4 tablespoons bottled white horseradish, drained

Place all the ingredients in the container of a blender or processor fitted with steel blade. Process for 1 minute. Scrape down the sides of the container with a rubber spatula and process for 30 seconds longer. Keep in a well-sealed container and allow to stand overnight before using.

Use as a spread on cold meat sandwiches; serve with meatloaf, cold shrimp, any cold seafood.

Makes approximately 1 cup.

• Brown-Sugar Mustard •

1 cup dry mustard	Dash of cayenne pepper
½ cup light-brown sugar	½ cup white vinegar
½ teaspoon dried marjoram	¼ cup olive oil
1 teaspoon salt	

Place all the ingredients in the container of a blender or processor fitted with steel blade. Process for 1 minute. Scrape down the sides of the container with a rubber spatula and process for 30 seconds longer. Keep in a well-sealed container and allow to stand overnight before using.

Serve with hot or cold baked ham, sausages of any kind. Also use as a glaze when baking ham, tongue, or corned beef.

Makes approximately 1 cup.

• Spicy Mustard •

1 cup cider vinegar	1 teaspoon salt
4 whole cloves	2 tablespoons honey
4 peppercorns	2 tablespoons light-brown sugar
1 bay leaf	
4 juniper berries	¼ teaspoon ground ginger
1 cup dry mustard	¼ teaspoon ground cinnamon
1 tablespoon Worcestershire sauce	¼ teaspoon ground allspice

In a small saucepan bring to a boil over medium heat the cider vinegar, cloves, peppercorns, bay leaf, and juniper berries. Lower the heat and simmer for 5 minutes.

Place the dry mustard, Worcestershire sauce, salt, honey, light-brown sugar, ginger, cinnamon, and allspice in the container of a blender or processor fitted with steel blade. Strain the boiled mixture and add to the container. Process for 1 minute. Scrape down the sides of the container with a rubber spatula and process for 30 seconds longer. Mixture may seem thin. Keep in a well-sealed container and allow to stand overnight to thicken before using.

Serve with pâtés, pork, and ham dishes.

Makes approximately 1¼ cups.

• Tomato-Herb Mustard •

---

1 cup dry mustard	1 tablespoon
1 teaspoon salt	Worcestershire sauce
4 tablespoons red wine	1 tablespoon dried basil
vinegar	leaves
4 tablespoons dry red wine	4 tablespoons tomato paste

Place all the ingredients in the container of a blender or processor fitted with steel blade. Process for 1 minute. Scrape down the sides of the container with a rubber spatula and process for 30 seconds longer. Keep in a well-sealed container and allow to stand overnight before using.

Add to taste in beef or lamb stews; add to marinades. Serve as a condiment with barbecued chicken, beef, or pork.

Makes approximately 1¼ cups.

• Russian Mustard •

---

1 cup dry mustard	3 tablespoons white vinegar
2 tablespoons cold water	2 tablespoons vegetable oil
1½ cups boiling water	½ teaspoon salt
¾ cup granulated sugar	

In a bowl mix together the dry mustard and cold water to form a stiff paste. Smooth down the mixture with a rubber spatula.

Pour ½ cup of the boiling water over the mustard; do not stir. Let the water sit on top. Allow to cool and carefully pour the water off. Pour another ½ cup of boiling water over the mustard and repeat the procedure. Repeat once more with the last ½ cup. When this last is cooled and poured off, whisk in the sugar, vinegar, oil, and salt. Blend well. Keep in a well-sealed container and allow to stand overnight before using.

Serve with Siberian Dumplings (page 105), broiled fish, cold vegetables. Add to taste to vegetable soups.

Makes approximately 1¼ cups.

• Coarse-Ground Mustard •

¼ cup white or brown
  mustard seeds
¼ cup red wine vinegar
¼ cup dry red wine

½ cup dry mustard
2 teaspoons salt
¼ teaspoon ground allspice
2 tablespoons cold water

Place the mustard seeds, wine vinegar, and wine in a small bowl and let stand for 3 hours. Pour both the seeds and the liquid into the container of a blender or processor fitted with steel blade. Process with several on-off motions until the seeds are bruised and broken. Add the dry mustard, salt, allspice, and water and process for 30 seconds. Scrape down the sides of the container with a rubber spatula and process for 30 seconds longer. Keep in a well-sealed container and allow to stand overnight before using.

Use as a table mustard for all meat dishes, pâtés, sausages, and as a sandwich spread.

Makes approximately 1 cup.

½ cup dry mustard	2 teaspoons Worcestershire
½ cup granulated sugar	sauce
¼ cup boiling water	½ teaspoon salt
2 tablespoons vegetable oil	2 teaspoons cider vinegar

Place all the ingredients in the container of a blender or processor fitted with steel blade. Process for 1 minute. Scrape down the sides of the container with a rubber spatula and process for 30 seconds longer. Keep in a well-sealed container and allow to stand overnight before using.

Serve as an accompaniment to cold or hot seafood dishes, cold meats, smoked fish.

Makes approximately ¾ cup.

GROWING MUSTARD SPROUTS

Mustard sprouts, which are not available in the markets, are easily grown at home. Choose a sunny window and follow these instructions:

To grow mustard sprouts:

METHOD I   Fill a flat clay saucer or shallow pot about 6 inches in diameter with damp soil. Scatter white mustard seeds liberally over the soil. Cover with a thin layer of dry soil. Place on a sunny windowsill. In two days sprouts will begin to appear. In four days it will be harvest time. Cut as much greenery as you will need for salads or sandwiches.

METHOD II   Soak a double layer of paper towels in water and wring out excess moisture. Lay the paper towels in the bottom of a shallow dish and sprinkle the seeds evenly over the surface. Cover with another layer of moist paper towels to keep seeds damp. Whenever top layer of towels seems dry, spray or sprinkle lightly with more water. You may start seeing life in twenty-four hours. In a few days the sprouts will have grown to eating size. Rinse and drain before using.

They have a fresh, pungent, mustardy taste that is a super addition to salads and sandwiches. The seeds will sprout in two days and be ready for harvest in four days.

Extra sprouts can be stored in a well-sealed plastic bag in the refrigerator. They will keep for up to a week without losing their flavor. You may eat the entire sprout, including the stems, hulls, and roots.

APPETIZERS AND FIRST COURSES

• Flaky Ham Crescents •

½ cup butter, at room
temperature
¼ pound cream cheese, at
room temperature
4 tablespoons Dijon
mustard

1 cup all-purpose flour
¼ pound prosciutto ham,*
thinly sliced
1 egg white, mixed with
1 tablespoon cold water

Place the butter and cream cheese in a bowl and blend together with a wooden spoon. Add the mustard, creaming it in thoroughly. Add the flour and continue to work in with the spoon until a dough is formed and leaves the sides of the bowl cleanly.

Dough may be made in a processor fitted with steel blade. Cut the butter and the cream cheese into small pieces. Place in the container of the processor along with the mustard and flour. Process the mixture with several quick on-off motions until ingredients are combined. Then, with motor running, process for 1 minute longer until the dough forms a ball and leaves the sides of the container.

Shape the dough into 2 equal balls, flatten, and wrap each half in waxed paper. Refrigerate for 2 hours.

Preheat oven to 350 degrees.

On a floured surface, roll out each flattened ball of dough

*Available at Italian food specialty stores, or substitute smoked ham.

into a circle ⅛-inch thick, approximately 8 inches in diameter. Divide the amount of prosciutto in half and cover the surface of each circle entirely. Using a sharp knife and cutting through both the ham and pastry, divide the circle into 16 triangles (first by halving the circle, then quartering, etc.). Roll up each triangle starting with the wide end, working toward the point. Turn the ends in toward each other to form crescent shapes.

Place the crescents on an ungreased baking sheet, with the point of the triangle tucked under. Brush with the egg-white mixture and bake for 20 minutes or until golden.

Makes 32 small crescents.

NOTE: The baked crescents will keep refrigerated for several days. To reheat, bake at 350 degrees for 5 minutes. They can also be frozen for up to 6 weeks. Reheat, frozen, in a 400-degree oven for 10 minutes.

• Steak Tartare •

2 pounds lean ground sirloin (trimmed weight)
4 egg yolks
1 medium onion, finely chopped
3 teaspoons salt
3 tablespoons chopped fresh parsley
1 large clove garlic, minced
3 tablespoons Dijon mustard
1 tablespoon Worcestershire sauce
1 2-ounce can flat anchovy fillets, drained and chopped
2 tablespoons capers, drained
1 tablespoon cognac
Freshly ground black pepper to taste

Have the butcher trim the meat of all fat and grind it twice. You can do this step yourself if your food processor grinds meat evenly. Use the steel blade.

Put the ground meat into a large mixing bowl along with the egg yolks, onion, salt, parsley, garlic, mustard, Worcestershire sauce, anchovy fillets, capers and cognac.

Mix all the ingredients thoroughly, either with your

hands or by using two knives, pulling the knives in opposite directions, turning the bowl frequently as you work. When all the ingredients are well combined, shape into a loaf and refrigerate until serving.

Serve on a platter garnished with watercress and a lattice topping of additional flat anchovies. Sprinkle with additional capers and lots of freshly ground pepper. Serve with thinly sliced triangles of pumpernickel.

Serves at least twenty at a buffet, or six to eight as a first course.

• Carpaccio •

1 pound filet of beef	1 tablespoon lemon juice
2 egg yolks	¼ cup chicken stock
1 teaspoon dry mustard	½ teaspoon salt
¼ cup peanut oil	Capers
1 tablespoon Dijon mustard	Chopped fresh parsley
1 teaspoon Worcestershire sauce	Freshly ground black pepper

Slice the raw beef paper-thin. Freezing the filet for an hour will help make this easy. The sliced beef will defrost rapidly.

Place the egg yolks and dry mustard in the container of a blender or processor fitted with steel blade. Process for 1 minute until slightly thickened. Gradually add the oil, drop by drop, as in making mayonnaise. When all the oil is added, add the prepared mustard, Worcestershire sauce, lemon juice, chicken stock, and salt, and process for 30 seconds longer. The sauce will be the consistency of thin mayonnaise.

Arrange the beef slices, divided equally, on six individual plates. The number of slices will depend upon your slicing expertise. Coat the slices with the sauce and garnish with capers, parsley, and generous quantities of freshly ground pepper.

Serves six.

• Beef Rolls •

¼ pound air-cured beef, thinly sliced (rollfleisch or bunderfleisch)*
½ pound cream cheese, softened
2 teaspoons sour cream
1 teaspoon bottled white horseradish, drained
1 tablespoon Dijon mustard
1 teaspoon Worcestershire sauce
1 tablespoon chopped fresh parsley
Additional chopped parsley for garnish

In a small bowl, cream the cheese with the sour cream, horseradish, mustard, Worcestershire sauce, and parsley, using a wooden spoon, until smooth.

Spread this mixture evenly over the slices of beef, being sure to bring the filling out to the long edges of the beef.

Roll the slices up from the short end, jelly-roll style, and chill the rolls for 1 hour. Cut them crosswise to about 1½ inches in length. This will again depend upon the size of the rolls. Dip the cut ends in the chopped parsley.

Serves ten to twelve.

*Available at German delicatessens.

• Blender Pâté •

1 medium onion, cut into large chunks
1 large clove garlic
2 eggs
¾ pound chicken livers
¼ pound sweet Italian sausage meat
Several sprigs of fresh parsley
¼ cup flour
½ teaspoon dried thyme leaves
½ teaspoon ground ginger
½ teaspoon ground allspice
Pinch of ground nutmeg
1 tablespoon salt
1 teaspoon freshly ground black pepper
4 tablespoons butter, at room temperature
¾ cup heavy cream
2 tablespoons Dijon mustard
1 tablespoon cognac

Preheat oven to 325 degrees.

Place the onion, garlic, and eggs into the container of a blender or processor fitted with steel blade and process for 1 minute. Add the chicken livers, sausage meat, and parsley and use several quick on-off motions to coarsely chop. Add the flour, thyme, ginger, allspice, nutmeg, salt, pepper, butter, cream, mustard, and cognac and process until the mixture is smooth. Scrape down the sides of the container with a rubber spatula and process for 30 seconds longer. The mixture will be very thin.

Pour the mixture into a well-buttered one-quart baking dish or decorative mold and set it into a large shallow pan of hot water. Butter a sheet of tin foil large enough to loosely cover the top of the mold and place greased side down.

Bake for 3 hours. Remove from the oven, remove the tin foil, and lift the baking dish from the pan of water. Allow the pâté to cool completely on a cooling rack before unmolding. To unmold, run a sharp knife around the edge of the pâté, place serving dish over mold, and turn both upside down. Chill the pâté before serving. It will keep, refrigerated, for 2 days.

Serves eight to ten.

• Shrimp and Artichoke Hearts Remoulade •

1 pound medium shrimp
1 quart water
1 teaspoon salt
½ teaspoon dried thyme
  leaves
½ bay leaf
1 teaspoon white mustard
  seeds

1 teaspoon red wine vinegar
1 9-ounce package frozen
  artichoke hearts or 1
  14-ounce can, drained
Remoulade Sauce
Capers

Peel and devein the shrimp; rinse well. Place water, salt, thyme, bay leaf, mustard seeds, and wine vinegar in a large pot and bring to a boil over high heat. Add the shrimp and simmer for 3 to 5 minutes, until pink. Drain and set aside.

Cook the artichoke hearts according to directions on the package. Drain and set aside. If using canned artichoke hearts, drain and set aside.

Both the shrimp and artichoke hearts should be slightly chilled before mixing with the sauce. When ready, place the shrimp in a bowl, coat thoroughly with the sauce, and fold the artichoke hearts in carefully. Refrigerate for several hours before serving.

Serve on individual plates on a bed of watercress; sprinkle with additional whole capers.

Serves six.

REMOULADE SAUCE

1 cup mayonnaise
¼ cup Creole mustard or Dijon mustard
½ teaspoon anchovy paste
1 teaspoon lemon juice
2 scallions, greens included, finely chopped
2 tablespoons chopped fresh parsley
1 tablespoon sweet gherkins, finely chopped
1 tablespoon capers, drained, finely chopped
½ teaspoon dried tarragon leaves

In a small bowl whisk together the mayonnaise, mustard, anchovy paste, and lemon juice until well combined. Fold in the scallions, parsley, gherkins, capers, and tarragon.

Makes about 1½ cups.

NOTE: Use remoulade sauce with cooked cold shellfish such as mussels and scallops; with raw clams, fried seafood, or as a dip for raw vegetables.

• Crabmeat and Avocado Remoulade •

1 pound cooked lump
   crabmeat
1 large ripe avocado

Remoulade sauce
Pimientos

Pick over the crabmeat and discard any cartilage. Peel and cut the avocado into medium-sized cubes. Place the crabmeat in a bowl; mix in the remoulade sauce, coating completely. Fold in the avocado gently, so as not to squash.

Serve on individual plates on a bed of watercress; garnish with strips of pimiento.

Serves six.

•Cotechino in Crust •

2 cotechino (Italian garlic
   sausage), about 1 pound
   each, or substitute any
   spicy garlic sausage such
   as Kielbasa
4 tablespoons Dijon

mustard with green
   peppercorns
1 recipe Short-Pastry
   Dough (page 214)
1 egg, beaten with 1 tablespoon cold water

Prick the surface of the sausages with a fork. Place in a large pot with water to cover. Bring to a boil over high heat, turn heat to low, and simmer, covered, for 1 hour. Drain the sausages, and when cool enough to handle, remove the casings. Cool completely before continuing.

When cooled, spread each sausage with 2 tablespoons of the mustard. Set aside while rolling out the prepared pastry.

Preheat oven to 400 degrees.

Roll out ¾ of the dough into one large rectangle ⅛-inch thick. With a sharp knife cut 2 even rectangles large enough to encase each sausage. Place one sausage in the center of one of the rectangles and bring the long sides up to overlap. Seal the seam by pressing together with fingertips. Bring the dough at the ends up and seal with fingertips. Repeat with second sausage. Place the two encased sausages seam-side down on an ungreased baking sheet. Brush the entire surface with the egg mixture. Roll out the remaining ¼ of the dough into a rectangle ⅛-inch thick. Cut into strips ½-inch wide with a pastry wheel or a sharp knife. Arrange the strips in a lattice pattern over the tops and sides of the two sausages and brush again with the egg mixture. Bake for 35 to 40 minutes, until browned.

Serve hot or cold with an assortment of mustards or with Herb Sauce (page 190) or bottled Mostarda di Cremona.*

Serves twelve.

*Mustard fruits, available at Italian food-specialty stores.

• Smoked-Salmon Mousse •

¼ pound smoked salmon, thinly sliced
½ cup butter, at room temperature
1 small onion, finely chopped
¼ teaspoon white pepper

1 tablespoon lemon juice
2 tablespoons Dijon mustard
½ cup heavy cream, whipped
2 tablespoons snipped fresh dill

In a small bowl, mash or chop the salmon to a paste. In another bowl, cream the butter and combine well with the salmon. Mix in the onion, pepper, lemon juice, and mustard until thoroughly blended. Fold in the whipped cream and the dill, again combining all ingredients thoroughly. When made in a processor fitted with steel blade, the procedure varies slightly. Place the sliced salmon in the container; process for a few seconds until it becomes a paste. Add the onion, which has been quartered; use a few quick on-off motions to chop it. Add the butter in small pieces, pepper, lemon juice, and mustard, and let the motor run for 1 minute until all the ingredients are combined. Scrape down the sides with a spatula and process a few seconds longer. Remove the salmon mixture to a bowl and fold in the whipped cream and dill with a rubber spatula until thoroughly mixed.

Pack the mixture into a well-buttered two-cup decorative mold (preferably fish-shaped) lined with a double layer of cheesecloth to facilitate the unmolding of the mousse. The cheesecloth should overhang several inches on each side of the mold. After filling the mold, fold the overhanging cheesecloth over the top of the mousse. Cover with plastic wrap and refrigerate overnight or at least 3 hours before serving.

To unmold, simply remove the plastic, fold back the cheesecloth, and place mold on a serving platter upside down. Lift the mold and carefully remove the cheesecloth from the mousse. Decorate with additional sprigs of fresh dill and serve with thinly sliced pumpernickel.

Makes approximately 1½ cups.

• Gravlax •

---

2 pounds fresh salmon (preferably center piece)
¼ cup coarse (kosher) salt
1 tablespoon sugar
1 tablespoon coarsely ground white pepper*
½ teaspoon coarsely

ground white mustard seeds*
½ teaspoon dry mustard
1 tablespoon cognac
3 large bunches fresh dill, approximately ¾ pound

Have the fish market split the piece of fish lengthwise and remove the center bone and any small bones as well. Leave the skin intact.

Wash and dry the salmon well.

In a small bowl, combine the salt, sugar, ground white pepper, ground mustard seeds, dry mustard, and cognac.

Rinse and dry the dill and lay one bunch in a glass or enamel dish large enough to hold the fish. Lay one side of

*Grind either by hand, with a mortar and pestle, or in a small electric coffee grinder.

---

the salmon on top, flesh side up, and sprinkle heavily with half of the salt mixture. Cover with the remaining two bunches of dill. Sprinkle the other side of the salmon (flesh side) with the remaining half of the salt mixture. Lay this piece on top of the dill, flesh side down, making a "sandwich" of the fish, with the dill and salt mixture in between. Cover the fish with waxed paper; place a weight such as a board or heavy platter on top. Place several canned goods or a 5-pound bag of flour or sugar on top for additional weight. Refrigerate for 3 days. Turn the complete fish sandwich every 12 hours; separate the layers each time and baste in between with the accumulated liquid. Replace weights and return to the refrigerator.

When serving, remove the fish from the marinade, scrape off the dill and salt mixture, and dry with paper towels. Slice the salmon in thin diagonal slices and serve with Mustard Dill Sauce (page 191) and thin slices of pumpernickel.

Serves eight to ten.

NOTE: The salmon will keep refrigerated for about a week. The same method of marinating can be applied to other fatty fish less expensive than salmon, such as herring or mackerel.

• Herring in Mustard Dill Sauce •

8 matjes herring fillets (about 1½ pounds)
1 cup spicy brown mustard
⅓ cup sugar
¾ cup vegetable oil

2 egg yolks
½ cup heavy cream
Large bunch fresh dill, finely snipped

In a shallow glass or enamel dish, soak the herring fillets in cold water and refrigerate for 24 hours, changing the water several times.

In a small bowl, whisk together the mustard and sugar until the sugar dissolves. Whisk in the oil gradually. Separately, beat the egg yolks with the cream and add to the mustard mixture. Mix well and fold in the dill.

When the herring fillets have soaked for the required length of time, rinse and pat them dry with paper towels. Cut each fillet crosswise into three pieces, place in a serving dish, and pour the mustard sauce over them. Toss the pieces to coat well and allow to marinate, refrigerated, at least two hours before serving.

Serves eight to ten.

• Deviled Crab •

1 pound fresh lump
   crabmeat
4 tablespoons butter
1 medium onion, finely
   chopped
½ green bell pepper, finely
   chopped
2 tablespoons Madeira wine
Salt and freshly ground
   black pepper to taste

¼ cup chopped fresh
   parsley
1 cup fresh bread crumbs
3 tablespoons Dijon
   mustard with red pepper
¼ cup heavy cream
1 cup Mustard Bread
   Crumbs (page 170)

Preheat oven to 350 degrees.

Pick over the crabmeat carefully; remove any bones or cartilage.

Melt 2 tablespoons of the butter in a skillet, add the onion and green pepper, and sauté over medium heat for 1 minute until soft. Stir in the crabmeat, add the Madeira, and raise the heat to high. Cook just until the liquid is absorbed. Season with salt and pepper.

Remove the pan from the heat and add the parsley, fresh bread crumbs, mustard, and cream. Mix together.

Divide the mixture among 8 well-buttered individual ramekins or scallop shells. Top each with a few spoonsful of the mustard bread crumbs. Melt the remaining 2 tablespoons of butter and drizzle over each dish.

Bake for 20 minutes or until browned.

Serves eight.

• Batter-Fried Butterfly Shrimp •

1 pound fresh large shrimp, uncooked	3 teaspoons baking powder
1 cup all-purpose flour	½ cup mustard oil*
1 cup cornstarch	1 to 1¼ cups cold water
	Peanut oil for deep frying

Peel the shrimp, leaving the tail segment on. Butterfly them by splitting each almost in two along the back. Remove the vein and lay them flat. Rinse and drain thoroughly on paper towels.

Place the flour, cornstarch, and baking powder in a bowl. Gradually whisk in the mustard oil. The batter will be quite thick. Start whisking in the water until the mixture thins, to the consistency of pancake batter.

In a deep fryer or deep pot heat the peanut oil to 375 degrees on a deep-fry thermometer. Dip the shrimp in the batter; add one at a time to the hot oil. Fry only 3 or 4 at a time, depending upon the size of the pot. Do not overcrowd. Fry for 2 or 3 minutes, turning to brown all sides. Drain on paper towels as they are done.

Serve with Mustard Soy Dipping Sauce (page 193).

Serves six.

*Available at Indian and oriental food-specialty stores.

• Batter-Fried Vegetables •

Using the same batter as in previous recipe, substitute raw vegetables such as turnips, green peppers, string beans, carrots, cauliflower, zucchini, or broccoli cut into bite-sized pieces. Fry as directed.

• Deviled Sardines •

2 cans (3¾ ounces each)
  sardines, skinless and
  boneless
2 tablespoons prepared hot
  English mustard
  (page 74)*
1 tablespoon lemon juice
1½ teaspoons
  Worcestershire sauce
Dash of Tabasco
8 slices buttered toast
1 cup fresh bread crumbs
2 tablespoons chopped
  fresh parsley

Preheat broiler to high.

Drain the sardines, reserving the oil from *one* can. In a small bowl, mash the sardines and mix in the reserved oil, mustard, lemon juice, Worcestershire sauce, and Tabasco.

Spread the mixture on the slices of buttered toast and cut each slice into thirds.

Mix together the bread crumbs and parsley and sprinkle on each slice. Place them on a baking sheet and broil for 2 minutes, being careful not to burn them.

Serve as appetizers on a tray garnished with watercress and lemon wedges. As a first course, slice each whole piece of toast diagonally in half; arrange on individual plates with garnish.

Serves eight.

*Or use prepared bottled hot English mustard.

• Sesame-Coated Chicken Wings •

2½ pounds chicken wings
½ cup Dijon mustard
1 tablespoon soy sauce
2 cloves garlic, crushed
½ teaspoon white pepper
2 eggs, beaten with
  2 tablespoons cold water
¾ cup flour
2 cups sesame seeds
Peanut oil for deep frying

Cut off and discard the wing tips from the chicken wings or reserve and freeze for making chicken stock. With a cleaver or sharp knife, halve the wings at the joints, rinse, and pat dry with paper towels.

In a small bowl mix together the mustard, soy sauce, garlic, and pepper. Place the chicken wing halves in a large bowl, pour the mustard mixture over them, and marinate for 2 hours at room temperature. Turn them occasionally and baste with the marinade.

Beat the eggs with the water in a bowl. Have the flour and sesame seeds ready on a large sheet of waxed paper. Dust the wings with the flour, dip in the egg, and coat completely with the sesame seeds. Place on a platter, cover with waxed paper, and refrigerate for 1 hour.

In a deep fryer or pot, heat the oil to 375 degrees on a deep-fat thermometer. Add the wing halves, a few at a time, and fry for about 6 to 8 minutes, turning them until golden brown. Drain on paper towels as they are done.

Serve hot or at room temperature with Mustard Soy Dipping Sauce (page 193).

Serves twelve or more.

• Marinated Mushrooms •

1 pound fresh mushrooms
½ cup mayonnaise
2 cloves garlic, crushed
2 tablespoons Dijon
mustard with green
peppercorns
Salt to taste

Rinse the mushrooms and pat dry with paper towels. Slice ⅛-inch thick and place in a serving bowl.

In a small bowl mix together the mayonnaise, garlic, and mustard. Toss with the sliced mushrooms to coat thoroughly. Chill for 1 hour, and toss again before serving.

Serve with sprigs of watercress.

Serves six to eight.

• Spicy Marinated Olives •

1 10-ounce jar large green
   unpitted olives
2 teaspoons dry mustard
½ cup olive oil
½ teaspoon dried oregano
   leaves

1 clove garlic, crushed
1 teaspoon hot red-pepper
   flakes

Drain the olives, reserving ¼ cup of their liquid. Set aside olives. Place the reserved liquid in a small bowl and whisk in the dry mustard until dissolved. Gradually whisk in the oil; add the oregano, garlic, and red-pepper flakes and mix thoroughly. Pour over the olives and pack into a well-sealed container. Refrigerate for at least 24 hours before serving.

• Artichoke Pie •

1 9-ounce package frozen
   artichoke hearts or 1
   14-ounce can, drained
2 tablespoons butter
3 eggs
15 ounces ricotta cheese
⅓ cup chopped fresh parsley
Salt and freshly ground
   black pepper to taste

¼ cup Dijon mustard
½ cup freshly grated
   Parmesan cheese
1 recipe Short-Pastry
   Dough (page 214)
¼ pound mozzarella
   cheese thinly sliced
1 egg, beaten with 1
   tablespoon water

Preheat oven to 400 degrees.

Allow the frozen artichoke hearts to partially thaw. Melt the butter in a skillet and sauté the artichoke hearts for 2 to 3 minutes over medium heat. Set aside. If using canned artichoke hearts, drain and sauté briefly. Set aside.

Beat the eggs in a bowl, add the ricotta, and continue beating until smooth. Add the parsley, salt, pepper, mustard, and Parmesan cheese and combine well.

Line a deep-dish 9-inch pie plate with half the pastry. Arrange the artichoke hearts on the pastry shell and pour the cheese filling over them. Layer the mozzarella on top and cover with the second circle of pastry. Seal the edges. Prick the entire surface of the dough with a fork to allow the steam to escape. Brush the surface with the beaten egg and water.

Bake for 15 minutes in the center of the oven, lower the oven heat to 325 degrees, and bake for an additional 45 to 55 minutes.

Serves eight.

• Stuffed Artichokes in Mustard Broth •

4 large artichokes
Water
Juice of 1 lemon

STUFFING

**2 tablespoons plus
4 teaspoons olive oil**
**1 small onion, finely
chopped**
Artichoke stems
**2 cloves garlic, finely
chopped**

1 cup fresh bread crumbs
**3 tablespoons chopped
fresh parsley**
**3 tablespoons freshly grated
Parmesan cheese**
**2 tablespoons Dijon
mustard with lemon**

BROTH

2 cups chicken stock
2 tablespoons olive oil
2 cloves garlic, whole

**Several sprigs of fresh
parsley**
1 tablespoon Dijon mustard

Cut off the artichoke stems, pare, chop fine, and reserve. Remove any tough, bruised outer leaves from the artichoke. Cut off the top one-fourth, and with a scissors, snip the points off all remaining leaves. Spread open the leaves, and

---

with a spoon, scrape out and discard all of the hairy choke within. Rinse the artichokes and plunge them into boiling salted water to which the lemon juice has been added. Cook covered, for 10 minutes over medium heat and drain upside down.

To make the stuffing, heat 2 tablespoons of the oil in a skillet, add the onion, reserved artichoke stems, and garlic, and sauté for 2 minutes over medium heat. Remove the pan from the heat and add the bread crumbs, parsley, Parmesan cheese, and mustard. Spread the leaves of the artichokes and fill the center cavity of each one with the stuffing.

Stand the stuffed artichokes in a wide pot; drizzle a teaspoon of olive oil over each. Pour the stock into the pot, add 2 tablespoons olive oil, garlic, and parsley, and bring the liquid to a boil over high heat. Lower heat to simmer, cover the pot, and simmer for 40 minutes until the artichokes are done. Remove the pan from the heat; swirl the mustard into the broth. Let the artichokes stand in the broth until they are tepid. They are best when served at this temperature. Place in individual bowls and pour some of the broth in each for dipping.

Serves four.

• Scale down some of your favorite fast foods to miniature size to have with drinks. Make tiny roast-beef sandwiches with tissue-thin slices of roast beef on cocktail rye spread with Horseradish Mustard (page 74), and cut in half diagonally. Pan fry 1-inch diameter hamburgers, spread halved miniature round dinner rolls with Dijon mustard, sprinkle with minced onion. Top the tiny burgers with 1-inch squares of sliced cheese after you've flipped them over, and you have cheeseburgers. The point is, notice what's miniature-size on your grocer's bread shelf and let your imagination take over from there.

• Bacon-and-Tomato Bites •

2 pints ripe cherry tomatoes	½ cup Dijon mustard
1 cup mayonnaise	1 pound sliced bacon

Cut a small slice off the stem end of each tomato and scoop out the seeds with the point of a sharp knife or spoon, leaving an empty shell.

Mix together the mayonnaise and mustard and fill each tomato with about 1 teaspoon of the mixture.

Sauté the bacon until crisp. Drain on paper towels, and when cooled, crumble into small pieces. Top each filled tomato with a generous sprinkling of the bacon.

Makes about four dozen. A pint basket usually contains about two dozen tomatoes.

NOTE: Cherry tomatoes can be filled with the mayonnaise-mustard mixture ahead of serving time and refrigerated. Fry the bacon in advance, and crumble. Reheat briefly in a moderate oven just to crisp before sprinkling on tomatoes.

• Mustard Puffs •

1 cup cold water	4 eggs
½ cup butter, cut in pieces	1 cup (4 ounces) sharp
½ teaspoon salt	cheddar cheese, coarsely
⅛ teaspoon white pepper	grated
1 cup all-purpose flour, sifted	2 tablespoons Dusseldorf mustard

Preheat oven to 425 degrees.

Put the water, butter, salt, and pepper in a medium saucepan and bring to a boil over high heat, boiling until the butter melts.

Turn the heat to low, add the flour all at once, and stir

vigorously with a wooden spoon for 2 to 3 minutes until the mixture forms a ball and leaves the sides of the pan. Remove the pan from the heat.

Make a well in the center of the dough and break 1 egg into it. Beat into the dough for several seconds until it is absorbed. Repeat with the remaining eggs, one at a time, beating well after each addition. The dough will become stiffer with the addition of each egg. Beat in the cheese and the mustard until both are thoroughly incorporated.

Form the puffs by using two teaspoons to shape a ball, or use a pastry bag fitted with a large round tube. Bake the puffs placed 1 inch apart on a large baking sheet. Bake for 15 minutes and lower the oven heat to 375 degrees. Continue to bake for 10 minutes longer. They should be completely dry when done, with no drops of moisture showing. Remove the baking sheet from the oven and, with the point of a sharp knife, make several small slits in the puffs. This will allow any moisture to escape. Turn the oven heat off and return the puffs to the oven for 10 minutes to dry out.

Makes approximately 4 dozen puffs, 1¼ inches in diameter.

NOTE: The puffs will freeze, well-wrapped in plastic bags or containers, for up to two months. To reheat, place frozen puffs on a baking sheet in a preheated 425-degree oven for about 5 minutes.

• Deviled Eggs •

6 hard-cooked eggs
2 tablespoons Dijon
  mustard
2 tablespoons butter,
  softened

1 teaspoon Worcestershire
  sauce
1 teaspoon anchovy paste

Cut the eggs in half lengthwise and remove the yolks to a small bowl, being careful not to damage the whites.

Mash the yolks together with the mustard, butter, Worcestershire sauce, and anchovy paste. With a spoon, fill the whites with the egg-yolk mixture or pipe through a pastry tube fitted with a star tip. Garnish with either freshly chopped parsley, capers, or bits of pimiento.

Makes 12 stuffed egg halves.

• Use the Marinated Mushrooms recipe (page 93), chopping the mushrooms instead of slicing them, and fill cherry tomato cups as in Bacon-and-Tomato Bites, page 97.

• Slice open and fill Mustard Puffs (page 97) with a teaspoonful of leftover (slim chance) Blender Pâté (page 83); heat briefly in a preheated 425-degree oven.

• Mash a quantity of mustard sprouts together with cream cheese or soft cheddar to spread on crackers or sandwiches.

• Try creaming together equal parts of gorgonzola cheese and sweet butter; add Dijon mustard by the teaspoonful to taste. Spread on sliced Italian bread, bake in foil, and serve hot instead of garlic bread.

• As another change from garlic bread, try splitting a loaf of French bread lengthwise. Spread with Mustard Butter (page 193), sprinkle with chopped scallions and parsley, and heat in the oven.

• Spread triangles of thinly sliced pumpernickel with soft Cheddar-cheesespread mixed with Dijon mustard and crushed fresh garlic. Top with curls of anchovy. Serve with drinks.

• Dress melon balls with lemon juice mixed with a little powdered mustard and powdered ginger—an indefinable improvement on nature.

• For finger foods with drinks, coat lengths of blanched asparagus with Mustard Mayonnaise (page 192) and roll up with thin slices of smoked ham. Offer more Mustard Mayonnaise for dipping.

• Brush phyllo leaves with melted Mustard Butter (page 193) before filling with spinach, seafood, meat, or chicken.

• Substitute *fresh* English made-mustard for Tabasco and turn a Bloody Mary into a Musty Mary. Try it, too, with homemade horseradish mustard (page 74). Use about 1 teaspoonful to 8 ounces of tomato juice or to taste.

• Spice up a tomato juice cocktail with a little Dijon mustard and a touch of half-and-half. Decorate with a parsley sprig.

• Add spicy brown mustard to sauerkraut for a Reuben Sandwich. Spread more on slices of rye or pumpernickel, assemble sandwich, and brown on both sides in clarified butter till Swiss cheese melts and corned beef heats through.

• The famous French ham-and-melted-cheese sandwich, *Croque Monsieur,* takes on a Burgundian lilt when the bread is spread with Dijon green peppercorn mustard before the assemby and final sautéing in clarified butter.

SOUPS

• Cream of Mustard Soup •

1 whole chicken breast
with skin and ribs
attached, split in half
4 to 5 cups chicken stock
2 tablespoons butter
1 tablespoon flour
1 tablespoon dry mustard
2 egg yolks

1 cup heavy cream
Salt and white pepper to
taste
2 tablespoons Dijon
mustard
3 scallions, green included,
finely chopped

Place the chicken-breast halves in a saucepan with 3 cups of the chicken stock. Bring the liquid to a boil over high heat, lower the heat, and simmer, covered, for 25 minutes. Allow the chicken to cool in the stock. When cooled, remove the meat from the breasts and discard the skin and bones. Slice the chicken meat into strips and reserve.

Strain the cooking liquid and add enough stock to it to make 4 cups. Place the stock in a saucepan, bring to a boil, and keep warm over low heat.

In another saucepan, melt the butter and whisk in the flour and dry mustard over low heat for 1 minute. Pour in the hot stock, slowly, whisking as you add. Beat the egg yolks in a small bowl with the cream, salt, and pepper. Add a little of the hot liquid to the cream mixture, then pour the cream mixture into the stock. Whisk over low heat for 5 minutes. Add more stock at this point if soup is too thick. Remove the pan from the heat and whisk in the mustard.

Serve the soup in individual bowls topped with sliced

---

chicken and the scallions, or chill for several hours. Serve cold with cold sliced chicken or other toppings such as tiny cold cooked shrimp, chopped watercress, or chopped cucumbers.

Serves six.

• Broccoli Soup •

---

1 bunch broccoli
4 cups chicken stock
1 cup plain yogurt
2 raw egg yolks

1½ tablespoons Dijon
mustard with lemon
Salt and freshly ground
black pepper to taste

Wash the broccoli well; cut off and discard the lower tough ends of the stems. Slice the remaining stems into ½-inch pieces and break buds into small flowers. Simmer the broccoli and stock in a saucepan for about 20 minutes or until the stem pieces are tender. Cool slightly in the liquid.

Set aside one cup of the broccoli flowers, and in a blender or a processor fitted with steel blade, puree the broccoli and stock for 2 minutes until smooth. Puree several cups at a time and pour back into the saucepan.

In a small bowl beat the yogurt with the egg yolks and mustard. Pour into the broccoli soup, add salt and pepper, and heat over a medium flame for 5 minutes. If the soup is too thick for your taste, add more stock at this point. Serve with the reserved broccoli flowers.

Serve the soup hot or chilled.

Serves six to eight.

• Mushroom Barley Soup •

1 cup pearl barley
12 cups chicken stock
4 tablespoons Dijon
    mustard
2 tablespoons butter
1 large onion, coarsely
    chopped
2 celery stalks, coarsely
    chopped

3 carrots, coarsely chopped
1 large clove garlic, minced
¼ pound fresh mushrooms,
    chopped
2 tablespoons chopped
    fresh parsley
4 tablespoons snipped fresh
    dill
Chopped scallions

In a medium-sized saucepan combine the barley with 2 cups of the chicken stock; bring to a boil over medium heat. Reduce the heat to low and cook, covered, until the liquid is absorbed, about 25 minutes. Remove the pan from the heat, stir in the mustard, and set aside.

In a stockpot, melt the butter, add the onion, celery, carrots, garlic, mushrooms, and parsley and cook for 10 minutes over low heat until the vegetables are softened. Add the additional 10 cups of stock and the reserved barley and bring to a boil over high heat. Cover, reduce heat to low, and simmer for 30 minutes. Taste for seasoning and add salt and pepper if necessary.

Stir in the dill before serving and sprinkle a handful of chopped scallions into each bowl.

Makes approximately 12 cups.

• Split-Pea Soup •

1 pound green split peas
2 tablespoons butter
2 celery stalks, coarsely
  chopped
1 leek, trimmed, coarsely
  chopped
2 carrots, scraped, coarsely
  chopped
1 large onion, coarsely
  chopped
1 medium potato, peeled,
  diced into small pieces
1 large clove garlic, finely
  minced

¼ cup chopped fresh
  parsley
2 teaspoons salt
Freshly ground black
  pepper to taste
Ham bone with ample meat
  attached (from baked
  smoked ham)
1 bay leaf, split in half
3 quarts cold water
3 tablespoons Dijon
  mustard

Soak the split peas for 12 hours or overnight in cold water to cover. Drain.

In a large stockpot, melt the butter and add the celery, leek, carrots, onion, potato, garlic, parsley, salt, and pepper. Cook the vegetables slowly in the butter for 10 minutes over medium heat.

Add the peas, ham bone, bay leaf, and the 3 quarts of cold water. Raise the heat to high, bring the liquid to a boil, cover, lower the heat, and simmer for 3 hours.

Cool the soup, remove the bone, and dice the meat, trimming it of all fat. Reserve the meat. Remove and discard the bay leaf. Puree the soup, a few cups at a time, in a blender or processor fitted with steel blade. Return the soup to the pot, whisk in the mustard, and taste for seasoning. Add the diced meat to the soup and heat through for several minutes.

Makes approximately 15 cups.

• Siberian Dumplings in Broth •

Dumplings
2 quarts chicken stock
Bunch of fresh dill, finely
  snipped

Sour cream
Russian Mustard (page 76)

DUMPLING DOUGH
1½ cups all-purpose flour
½ teaspoon salt

2 eggs
2 tablespoons cold water

Sift the flour and salt together into a large bowl. Make a well in the center and place the eggs and water in it. Work in the flour with fingers to form a dough. Turn out onto a lightly floured surface and knead for several minutes until the dough is smooth and elastic. Cover with a towel and allow to rest while preparing the filling.

FILLING
3 tablespoons vegetable oil
1 small onion, finely
  chopped
½ pound ground lean beef
½ pound ground veal
Salt and white pepper to
  taste

⅛ teaspoon ground nutmeg
2 tablespoons sour cream
2 tablespoons snipped fresh
  dill

Heat the oil in a skillet, add the onion, and cook over low heat for 5 minutes. Add the meat and continue to cook for 10 minutes longer, stirring frequently. Season with salt, pepper, and nutmeg. Remove the pan from the heat and allow to cool slightly. Stir in the sour cream and dill. Set aside.

On a lightly floured surface, with a lightly floured rolling pin, roll the dough out as thin as possible to form a large rectangle, about 12 inches by 18 inches. With a sharp knife or pastry wheel, cut the dough into 3-inch squares. Place about 1 tablespoon of the filling on each square. Fold the dough over to form a triangle. Press the edges firmly together with fingertips to seal, or press with a pastry crimper. Makes approximately 24 dumplings.

In a large pot bring the chicken stock to a boil over high heat. Drop in the filled dumplings, lower to medium heat, and cook gently, covered, for 20 minutes. Transfer the dumplings with a slotted spoon to warm individual soup bowls and ladle the stock over them. Place a generous spoonful of the fresh dill in each bowl. Pass a dish of sour cream and a dish of the Russian mustard so that each individual can stir in as much or as little into the broth as desired. This creates a sauce for the dumplings right in the bowl.

Serves four.

• To enliven hot creamed-potato soup, puree mustard sprouts with a cup of the hot soup, pour back into the pot, heat, stirring, and serve with more sprouts as garnish.

• A dollop of mustard-flavored sour cream does wonderful things for an icy bowl of borscht or vichyssoise.

• Swirl one teaspoon of Dijon mustard into a steaming bowl of cream of tomato or pea soup just before serving, to add an indefinable piquancy.

• A little dry mustard added to creamed soups gives them an interesting edge. Add by the teaspoonful to taste.

ENTREES: MEATS

• Crusty Roast Beef •

---

3 pounds beef for roasting
  (eye round, top sirloin,
  or sirloin tip)
2 teaspoons dry mustard
¼ cup Dijon mustard

2 cloves garlic, crushed
1 tablespoon soy sauce
1 tablespoon olive oil
1 medium onion, thinly
  sliced

Rub the dry mustard into entire surface of the roast.

In a small bowl, whisk together the Dijon mustard, garlic, soy sauce, and oil. Smear this liberally to cover the roast. Place the meat, fat side up, in a roasting pan, on top of onion slices. Allow to stand at room temperature for 2 hours before roasting.

Preheat oven to 500 degrees.

Roast meat at high temperature for 15 minutes. Lower oven heat to 350 degrees and continue roasting for an additional 45 minutes for rare beef. Let the meat rest for about 10 minutes before carving, to allow the juices to settle. Keep warm by making a loose tent with a sheet of aluminum foil. If using a meat thermometer it should register 120 for rare beef, 130 for medium rare, and 150 for well done.

Serves six.

NOTE: Use this mustard coating on roast lamb or pork. Add fresh or dried herbs to the mustard mixture, rosemary or basil with pork, thyme or mint with lamb.

4 tablespoons vegetable oil
1½ cups onions, finely chopped
1 large clove garlic, finely minced
1 pound (3 medium) cold boiled potatoes, diced into small pieces
1½ pounds cold roast beef, diced into small pieces
1½ tablespoons Worcestershire sauce
2 tablespoons chopped fresh parsley
4 tablespoons prepared hot English mustard (page 74)*
Salt and freshly ground black pepper to taste
½ cup beef stock

Preheat oven to 350 degrees.

In a large skillet heat the oil; add the onions and garlic and sauté over medium heat for about 5 minutes until transparent.

Add the potatoes and cook for several minutes longer, until they begin to brown. Add the roast beef, mix well; add the Worcestershire sauce, parsley, mustard, salt and pepper. Continue to cook until ingredients are just heated through.

Pour in the stock, raise heat to high, and cook for a minute longer until the liquid evaporates. Scrape up all browned particles sticking to the pan with a wooden spoon. Remove pan from the heat.

Have ready a rectangular baking pan, 9 × 13 × 2 inches, well greased with oil. Turn the hash into the pan, making an even layer, and bake for 20 minutes. The hash will become crusty and browned. If desired, run the pan under a hot broiler to brown even more.

Serves four.

NOTE: Hash may also be baked in individual gratin dishes. Optional: Top each serving with a poached egg.

*Or use prepared bottled hot English mustard.

• Corned Beef Hash •

Follow the directions for the roast beef hash in the preceding recipe, substituting cold corned beef for the roast beef. Try a Dusseldorf mustard instead of the English. Optional: add 1 small green pepper, finely chopped.
Serves four.

• Glazed Corned Beef •

6 pounds corned brisket of beef	6 peppercorns
	Cloves
1 bay leaf, split in half	Beer Glaze-recipe follows

Rinse the meat thoroughly under cold running water. Place in a large pot with cold water to cover. Add the bay leaf and peppercorns. Bring the liquid to a boil over high heat, skim off any fat, and reduce the heat to low. Simmer, covered, for 3 hours. Allow the meat to cool in the liquid to room temperature. Drain.

While the corned beef is cooking, prepare the glaze.

Preheat oven to 375 degrees.

Place the meat in a roasting pan, fat side up. Score the fat diagonally with a sharp knife making ⅛-inch deep incisions to create a diamond pattern. Stud the center of each diamond with a clove. Spoon some of the glaze over the meat to coat the fat completely, and bake for 30 minutes. Baste several times with additional glaze until it is used up. Serve with Pickled Mustard Sauce (page 190) and/or a variety of mustards.

Serves six to eight.

NOTE: Corned beef may be cooked in advance and refrigerated. Glaze and bake the next day.

BEER GLAZE

1 cup dark-brown sugar, firmly packed
4 teaspoons dry mustard
1 teaspoon bottled white horseradish, drained
¼ cup beer

In a small saucepan combine the brown sugar, dry mustard, horseradish, and beer and cook over low heat, stirring, for 5 minutes until the mixture is syrupy.

Makes approximately ½ cup.

• Beef Stroganoff •

1½ pounds boneless sirloin or filet of beef
Salt and freshly ground black pepper
4 tablespoons butter
2 tablespoons vegetable oil
1 medium onion, thinly sliced
½ pound mushrooms, sliced
1 tablespoon flour
1 cup beef stock
2 tablespoons Dijon mustard
½ cup sour cream
2 tablespoons snipped fresh dill

Slice the beef into thin strips. Season with salt and pepper and allow to stand for several hours in the refrigerator.

Melt 2 tablespoons of butter with the oil in a large skillet. Add the onion and sauté over medium heat for about 5 minutes or until onion is lightly browned. Add beef slices, raise heat to high, and brown meat for 1 minute on each side. Add mushrooms; sauté for 1 minute longer. Transfer ingredients to a warm platter.

In the same skillet, melt the remaining 2 tablespoons of butter over medium heat and add the flour, stirring with a wooden spoon. Pour in the stock; continue to stir until the sauce thickens. Add the mustard and stir until sauce is smooth. Return the onion, meat, and mushrooms to the pan, toss to coat with the sauce, and simmer for a few minutes. Add the sour cream. Stir and heat through, but do not boil, or the sour cream will curdle. Sprinkle with the dill and serve immediately.

Serves four.

• Mustard Carbonnade •

---

3 pounds bottom-round roast
3 tablespoons vegetable oil
4 cups thinly sliced onions
3 cloves garlic, finely minced
Salt and freshly ground black pepper to taste
1 teaspoon dried thyme leaves
1 bay leaf, split in half
1 cup beef stock
1½ cups beer
¼ cup chopped fresh parsley
¾ cup Dijon mustard
2 cups thinly sliced carrot rounds
Optional: ½ pound sliced mushrooms

In a deep heavy pot, heat the oil and sear the meat over high heat, turning to brown all sides. Remove the meat to a platter.

To the same oil, add the onions and garlic and cook slowly over medium heat for 10 minutes until lightly browned. Return the meat to the pot, add the salt, pepper, thyme, bay leaf, stock, beer, and parsley. Bring the liquid to a boil over high heat, reduce the heat to low, and simmer, covered, for 1 hour.

Transfer the meat to a carving board; slice with the grain, ¼-inch thick. Whisk the mustard into the cooking liquid and return the sliced meat to the pot along with the meat juices from the carving board. Add the carrots, cover, and continue to simmer for an additional 1½ hours or until the meat is fork tender. Taste and adjust the seasoning, if necessary. If you wish, mushrooms may be added for the last 10 minutes of cooking. Optional: Serve with Mustard Dumplings (page 217) added to the gravy during the last 20 minutes of cooking.

Serves six.

• Beef Curry •

2 pounds top-round beef
1 cup plain yogurt
2 tablespoons lemon juice
4 tablespoons clarified butter (page 217)
2 tablespoons brown mustard seeds*
1 medium onion, coarsely chopped
1 clove garlic, finely minced
1 teaspoon ground turmeric
1 teaspoon dry mustard
½ teaspoon hot red-pepper flakes
1 tablespoon finely minced fresh ginger root
1 teaspoon garam masala*
¼ cup chopped fresh cilantro (Chinese parsley)**
Salt and freshly ground black pepper to taste
½ cup beef stock

Trim the beef of all fat and cut into 1-inch cubes. Place the cubed beef in a large bowl, add the yogurt and lemon juice, and mix thoroughly. Marinate at room temperature for 1 hour. Turn occasionally to be sure all surfaces are coated with the marinade.

Heat the clarified butter in a large pot. When sizzling, add the mustard seeds, cover the pot, and allow the seeds to pop, about 1 minute, over medium heat. Remove the lid, add the onion and garlic, and sauté, stirring, for about 5 minutes, until golden. Add the beef cubes and yogurt marinade, turmeric, dry mustard, red-pepper flakes, ginger root, garam masala, cilantro, salt, and pepper, and continue to cook for 10 minutes, stirring occasionally. Add the stock; bring the liquid to a boil over high heat. Turn heat to low and simmer for 1 hour, or until the meat is tender.

Serves four.

*Available at Indian food specialty stores and health-food stores. Garam masala is a blend of hot spices, giving a distinctive flavor to many Indian dishes. The spices include cinnamon, cardamom, cloves, cumin, coriander, black peppercorns, and nutmeg. If unavailable substitute curry powder; however, do not expect the same results!
**Available at Spanish or oriental greengrocers.

• Beef Roulades •

2 pounds top-round steak
Salt and freshly ground
  black pepper to taste
8 teaspoons Dusseldorf
  mustard
8 tablespoons finely
  chopped onion
4 dill pickles, halved
  lengthwise

¼ cup flour
3 tablespoons vegetable oil
2 carrots, scraped, cut into
  thin rounds
1 cup beer
1 cup beef stock
Several sprigs of fresh
  parsley
1 bay leaf, split in half

Have the butcher cut the meat into ½-inch thick slices trimmed of all fat.

Cut the slices into 8 rectangles and place between two large sheets of waxed paper, pound them to ¼-inch thick with a metal meat pounder. Season lightly with salt and pepper. Spread each piece of meat with 1 teaspoon of mustard; sprinkle each with 1 tablespoon chopped onion. Place a strip of pickle on the narrow end of each piece and roll up tightly, jelly-roll fashion. Tie with butchers' twine at each end to secure well. Roll each piece in flour.

Heat the oil in a large skillet and add the beef rolls. Brown them on all sides over medium heat, about 5 minutes. Remove them to a platter and add the carrot rounds to the skillet. Sauté in the oil for 1 minute. Add the beer and beef stock, raise the heat to high, and boil for 1 minute. Return the rolls to the skillet along with the parsley and bay leaf. Lower heat, cover, and simmer for 1 hour. Remove the beef rolls to a platter. Transfer the cooking liquid and carrots to the container of a blender or processor fitted with steel blade. Discard the bay leaf. Process for 1 minute until carrots are just coarsely chopped. Pour the sauce back into the skillet and boil for 1 minute on high heat. Reduce heat to low, return the beef rolls to the sauce, and simmer for about 5 minutes.

Serves four.

• Marinated Flank Steak •

2 pounds flank steak, trimmed weight
4 tablespoons Dijon mustard
2 cloves garlic, crushed

2 tablespoons lemon juice
1 tablespoon soy sauce
½ cup olive oil
1 teaspoon dried oregano

Lightly score both sides of the steak to create a diamond pattern. This serves more than a decorative purpose; it will prevent the meat from curling as it broils.

Combine the mustard, garlic, lemon juice, and soy sauce in a small bowl. Whisk the oil in gradually until the marinade is creamy. Mix in the oregano.

Place the steak on a platter and brush both sides of the meat with the marinade, rubbing it into the incisions. Allow the meat to marinate for several hours before cooking, or marinate overnight in the refrigerator. If refrigerated, bring to room temperature before broiling.

Preheat broiler to high. Place the steak on a rack in broiling pan, reserving excess marinade. Broil for 5 minutes on each side for rare, longer for medium or well done. Baste with reserved marinade when turning the steak. The meat may be barbecued as well.

Serves four.

• Steak Salad •

2 pounds flank steak, marinated and broiled (see above)
1 sweet red onion, sliced, separated into rings

1 red bell pepper, seeded, cored, cut into strips
1 green bell pepper, seeded, cored, cut into strips
¼ pound fresh bean sprouts

Broil the steak in advance of preparing the salad so that the meat is at room temperature. Cut the broiled steak diagonally, against the grain, into thin slices; cut each slice in half crosswise.

Place the steak slices in a serving bowl together with the onion rings, pepper slices, and bean sprouts. Pour the dressing on, toss ingredients to mix, and allow to marinate at room temperature for 1 hour before serving.

Serves four to six.

DRESSING

¾ cup olive oil
1 large clove garlic
¼ cup rice wine vinegar
1 tablespoon soy sauce
2 tablespoons Dijon
  mustard

1 tablespoon lemon juice
Salt and freshly ground
  black pepper to taste
Several sprigs of fresh
  parsley

Place all the ingredients in the container of a blender or processor fitted with steel blade. Blend for 1 minute.

Makes 1 cup.

NOTE: Try the dressing over a salad of seasonal vegetables, blanched or raw, according to your preference.

• Steak Au Poivre in
Mustard Cream Sauce •

---

2 shell steaks, ¾-inch
  thick, well trimmed
  (reserve fat)
2 tablespoons coarse,
  freshly ground black
  pepper
2 tablespoons butter

2 shallots, finely chopped
2 tablespoons cognac
½ cup beef stock
½ cup heavy cream
2 tablespoons Dijon
  mustard
Chopped fresh parsley

Place the steaks on a large platter; season with the pepper, firmly pressing it with the heel of your hand into both sides of the steaks. Allow to stand for 1 hour at room temperature before cooking.

Rub a large skillet well with the reserved fat and sear the steaks over high heat for 1 minute on each side. Lower the

---

heat to medium and cook for 2 to 3 minutes longer on each side for rare; longer, depending upon desired doneness. Transfer the meat to a heated serving platter to keep warm.

Pour the fat from the pan; melt the butter over medium heat. Add the shallots and sauté for 1 minute, add the cognac, and ignite. Shaking the pan, cook until the flame dies.

Pour in the stock, increase the heat to high, and bring the liquid to a boil, scraping up particles from the pan with a wooden spoon. Add the cream and cook just until the sauce thickens.

Remove from the heat, swirl in the mustard, mixing well, pour over the steaks. Sprinkle with parsley and serve immediately.

Serves two.

NOTE: This dish may be cooked without the heavy cream addition as in the hamburger recipe that follows. Increase the amount of stock to ¾ cup and swirl in 2 tablespoons of butter at the end, along with the mustard.

• Hamburgers Au Poivre •

2 pounds ground beef, lean	2 tablespoons cognac
3 tablespoons coarse, freshly ground black pepper	1 cup beef stock
	4 tablespoons Dijon mustard
4 tablespoons butter	Chopped fresh parsley
4 shallots, finely chopped	

Shape the beef into 8 round patties and coat generously with the pepper on both sides, pressing the pepper into the meat with the heel of your hand. Allow to stand at room temperature for 1 hour before cooking.

Heat a large skillet, add the hamburgers, and cook over high heat for 1 minute on each side until the outside is crusty. Lower the heat to medium and cook for several minutes longer on each side, depending upon desired doneness. Transfer the hamburgers to a heated serving platter to keep warm.

Pour the fat from the pan, melt 2 tablespoons of the butter, and sauté the shallots over medium heat for 1 minute. Add the cognac, ignite, and cook, shaking the pan, until the flame dies.

Pour in the stock, raise the heat, and bring the liquid to a boil. Remove pan from the heat, swirl in the remaining 2 tablespoons of butter and the mustard, pour sauce over hamburgers. Sprinkle with parsley and serve immediately.

Serves four.

NOTE: The hamburgers may also be cooked with heavy cream, as in the preceding steak recipe. Decrease the amount of stock to ¾ cup, add ½ cup heavy cream, and omit the butter at the end.

• Meatloaf Diable •

2 pounds lean ground beef (sirloin or round)
1 large onion, coarsely grated
2 cloves garlic, crushed
Salt and freshly ground black pepper to taste
1 egg, well beaten
½ cup fresh bread crumbs
½ cup chopped fresh parsley
1 tablespoon Worcestershire sauce
¼ cup beef stock
4 tablespoons Dijon mustard

Preheat oven to 350 degrees.

In a large mixing bowl blend all the ingredients thoroughly. The best implement for mixing is your two hands. When everything is well mixed, shape into a loaf.

Place in a baking pan large enough to hold the loaf and bake for 1½ hours. Pour the fat from the pan and allow the meatloaf to rest for several minutes before serving. Serve cold, if you prefer. When served hot, a delicious accompaniment is Deviled Sauce I or II (pages 194 and 195).

Serves four.

• Deviled Roast Beef Bones •

4 roasted rib bones (left over from standing rib roast) with some meat attached	2 tablespoons red wine vinegar
½ cup butter	¼ cup Dijon mustard
	2½ to 3 cups fresh bread crumbs

Using the preparation method in the Deviled Country-Style Spareribs (page 133), coat the bones with the mustard mixture and bread crumbs. Refrigerate for 1 hour.

Preheat broiler to high.

Place the bones on a rack set in a shallow roasting pan. Broil about 3 or 4 inches away from the heat, for about 10 minutes. Turn several times to brown all sides; be careful not to burn. Serve with Deviled Sauce I or II (page 194 and 195).

Serves two or four, depending upon size and meatiness of bones.

NOTE: Roasted bones can be stockpiled in the freezer until you collect enough—one or two bones per person—to feed as many as you like.

• Deviled Short Ribs •

4 pounds short ribs of beef	2 tablespoons red wine vinegar
Salt and freshly ground black pepper to taste	¼ cup Dijon mustard
1 medium onion, sliced	2½ to 3 cups fresh bread crumbs
½ cup water	
½ cup butter	

Preheat oven to 500 degrees.

Season the ribs with salt and pepper. Arrange the sliced onion on the bottom of a roasting pan and lay the bones on top. Bake at high temperature for 15 minutes. Lower oven heat to 350 degrees, add the water to the pan, and continue to bake 30 minutes longer. (This may be done in advance, or the day before.)

Preheat broiler to high.

Cool the bones and coat with the mustard mixture and bread crumbs, as in Deviled Country-Style Spareribs (page 133). Place the bones on a rack set in a shallow roasting pan. Broil 10 minutes, about 3 or 4 inches away from the heat. Turn several times to brown all sides. Serve with Deviled Sauce I or II (pages 194 and 195).

Serves four.

• Veal Scaloppine Marsala •

1 pound veal scaloppine, thinly sliced	4 tablespoons butter
Salt and white pepper to taste	¼ cup Marsala wine
½ cup flour	½ cup beef stock
	1 tablespoon, grainy Dijon mustard

Have the butcher pound the scallopine very thin or pound it yourself with either a flat metal meat pounder or the wide blade of a meat cleaver.

Season the veal lightly with salt and pepper and coat both sides with the flour.

Heat the butter in a large skillet, and when sizzling, add the scallopine. Cook quickly over medium heat until golden, about 2 minutes on each side. Remove to a warm serving platter. Cover lightly with aluminum foil to keep warm.

Pour the Marsala into the pan, raise the heat to high, and cook, stirring up all browned particles from the pan with a wooden spoon. Cook until almost all the liquid is evaporated. Add the stock and boil for 1 minute, stirring. Remove the pan from the heat; swirl in the mustard. Pour the sauce over the scallopine and serve immediately.

Serves four.

• Vitello Mostarda •

2 tablespoons olive oil
3 pounds boned veal (rump or leg)
1 large onion, thinly sliced
2 carrots, scraped, thinly sliced
2 celery stalks, thinly sliced
2 large cloves garlic, finely minced
1 2-ounce can flat anchovy fillets, drained
1 cup dry white wine
½ cup chicken stock
Several sprigs of fresh parsley

1 large bay leaf, split in half
½ teaspoon dried thyme leaves
1 teaspoon salt
Freshly ground black pepper to taste
2 tablespoons white mustard seeds
1 cup mayonnaise
¼ cup Dijon mustard
1 tablespoon lemon juice
Capers
Chopped fresh parsley

Heat the oil in a pot large enough to contain the veal. Brown the meat over high heat, turning to brown all surfaces. Add the onion, carrots, celery, garlic, anchovy fillets, wine, stock, parsley sprigs, bay leaf, thyme, salt, pepper, and mustard seeds. Bring the liquid to a boil, lower the heat, and simmer, covered, for 2 hours.

Remove the veal from the pot and set aside to cool. Continue to cook the contents of the pot over medium heat for 10 minutes longer. Cool the sauce, discard the bay leaf, and puree the vegetables and liquid in a blender or processor fitted with steel blade. Remove the puree to a bowl and whisk in the mayonnaise, mustard, and lemon juice. Chill both the sauce and the veal for several hours before serving.

Serve the cold veal thinly sliced on a bed of fluffy cold rice. Sprinkle the veal with capers and chopped parsley. Pass the cold sauce separately.

Serves six to eight.

• Bratwurst in Mustard Beer •

8 bratwursts (German veal
   sausages)
3 cups light beer
¼ cup vegetable oil
4 cups thinly sliced onions
Salt and freshly ground
   black pepper to taste

2 tablespoons dark-brown
   sugar
½ cup flour
3 tablespoons Dusseldorf
   mustard

Prick the surfaces of the sausages with a fork, place them in a saucepan, and cover with the beer. Cook over medium heat for 10 minutes. Drain the sausages, reserving ¼ cup of the beer. Set aside the sausages and beer.

Heat the oil in a large skillet, add the onions, and slowly brown over low heat, about 10 minutes. Season with the salt, pepper, and brown sugar, and continue to cook for several minutes longer, until the onions begin to caramelize. Remove from the pan with a slotted spoon and reserve.

Dredge the sausages in flour, coating all sides well. Add to the fat in the skillet, raise the heat to high, and quickly brown the sausages on all sides. Pour in the reserved beer, swirl in the mustard, and cook for 2 minutes. Stir in the reserved onions and heat through. Serve immediately.

Serves four.

• Calves' Liver with Mustard Bread Crumbs •

1½ pounds calves' liver,
   ½-inch thick slices
Salt and white pepper to
   taste
½ cup flour
5 tablespoons butter
5 tablespoons vegetable oil

½ cup Dijon mustard
1 tablespoon chopped fresh
   parsley
1 teaspoon dried, crushed
   sage
3 cups fresh bread crumbs

Slice the liver into long strips about 1 inch wide. Season lightly with salt and pepper. Using a sheet of waxed paper on your work surface, dredge the strips in the flour, coating all surfaces.

Heat 2 tablespoons each of the butter and oil in a large skillet and quickly sauté the liver over high heat for 1 minute on each side to brown. Remove from the pan. Reserve pan for later use.

In a small bowl, thoroughly combine the mustard, parsley, and sage, and brush the liver slices with the mixture. Place bread crumbs on another sheet of waxed paper; roll slices in them, patting with fingers to make sure the coating adheres well. Refrigerate for 1 hour.

Wipe the reserved skillet dry with paper toweling; add the remaining 3 tablespoons each of the butter and oil. Heat, and when sizzling, sauté the breaded slices over medium heat for several minutes on each side, depending upon desired doneness.

Serves four.

• Using your favorite recipe, make several long, thin meat loaves (about 1½ inches in diameter), cool, and slice thin; serve on cocktail rye moistened with old-style grainy Dijon mustard—with cocktails.

• For a quick, delicious sauce for grilled ham steaks, combine a grated medium onion, 2 tablespoons of Dijon mustard, and 4 tablespoons of currant jelly. Spread over steaks after cooking, and run under broiler till sauce bubbles.

• Use fresh mustard sprouts as a garnish; they're a nice change from parsley.

• Tongue in Mustard
Vinegar Sauce •

2-pounds cooked cured   Mustard Vinegar Sauce
  tongue   ½ cup capers, drained

Place the tongue in a large pot with simmering water to cover. Cook, covered, for 30 minutes. Remove the tongue from its liquid and slice pieces about ⅛-inch thick. Place the slices in a skillet, cover with the sauce, and heat together over low heat for 10 minutes. Sprinkle with capers before serving.

Serves eight.

NOTE: Substitute baked ham slices for the tongue, and heat together with the sauce.

MUSTARD VINEGAR SAUCE

½ cup dry mustard   1 teaspoon Worcestershire
½ cup cider vinegar   sauce
¼ cup sugar   2 eggs
½ teaspoon salt   1 cup heavy cream

In a small saucepan whisk together the dry mustard and vinegar until smooth. Add the sugar, salt, Worcestershire sauce, and eggs, mixing thoroughly. Place over low heat and cook for 5 minutes, stirring constantly. Gradually whisk in the cream and continue to cook for several minutes longer until sauce thickens. Do not boil.

Makes approximately 1¼ cups.

NOTE: Serve the sauce cold with cold meats or cold seafood.

**½ leg of lamb about 3
pounds (boned weight)
Mint Marinade**

Have the butcher bone the meat, trim it of all fat, and pound it flat. It will be uneven in thickness and a little ragged-looking, but this won't matter after it's broiled.

Place the meat in a large shallow pan and cover completely with the marinade. Marinate in the refrigerator for 24 hours, turning occasionally and basting with the marinade. Remove from the refrigerator 2 hours before cooking and allow the meat to continue marinating at room temperature.

Preheat broiler to high.

Remove the meat from the marinade and broil about 4 inches from the heat for 15 minutes. Turn the meat, baste with additional marinade, and broil 15 minutes on second side. Serve immediately, cutting the meat diagonally against the grain. Lay the slices on a warm serving platter in an overlapping pattern. Serve with Mustard Mint Sauce (page 198).

Serves six.

MINT MARINADE

**½ cup Dijon mustard with
  lemon
1 cup dry red wine
2 cloves garlic, crushed
Freshly ground black
  pepper to taste**

**1 tablespoon salt
¼ cup olive oil
½ cup fresh mint leaves,
  coarsely chopped
1 medium onion, thinly
  sliced**

In a small bowl whisk together the mustard, wine, garlic, salt, and pepper. Gradually whisk in the oil. Add the mint leaves and the onion slices broken into rings.

Makes approximately 1½ cups.

• Currant-Glazed Country Ham •

One-half smoked ham,
either shank or butt end
(with rind), approximately
8 pounds

1 cup dry sherry
Cloves
Currant Glaze

Preheat oven to 300 degrees.

Rinse the ham well under cold running water, dry, and place in a roasting pan. Insert a meat thermometer into the thickest part of the meat. Pour the sherry over the ham and bake, uncovered, at about 20 minutes per pound. Ham, when done, should reach an internal temperature of 160 degrees on a meat thermometer.

While the ham is baking, prepare the glaze. One-half hour before the ham is done, remove it from the oven; cut away the rind with a sharp knife or kitchen shears. Score the fat diagonally ⅛-inch deep, to create a diamond pattern. Stud the center of each diamond with a clove. Spoon ⅓ of the glaze over the ham, reserving the rest to baste with. Raise the oven heat to 400 degrees; return the ham to the oven. Baste with the reserved glaze several times during the last one-half hour of baking. Serve the ham hot or at room temperature.

Serves eight to ten.

CURRANT GLAZE
1 cup red currant jelly
4 tablespoons dry sherry
2 teaspoons dry mustard

2 tablespoons Dijon
mustard

Melt the currant jelly and sherry in a small saucepan over low heat. When completely melted, remove the pan from the heat and whisk in both the dry and prepared mustard.

Makes approximately 1 cup.

• Roast Fresh Ham •

One-half fresh ham, either shank or butt end (with rind), approximately 8 pounds
1 large onion, sliced
Salt and white pepper to taste
Several cloves of garlic, to taste
1 cup dry sherry
Glaze

Preheat oven to 500 degrees.

Place the slices of onion in a large roasting pan. Rub the cut end of the ham with salt and pepper, make several incisions with a sharp knife, and insert whole or slivered garlic in the meat. Place the ham on top of the onions, covering them completely. Insert a meat thermometer into the thickest part of the meat. Bake for 20 minutes.

Lower the oven heat to 325 degrees, pour the sherry over the roast, and continue to bake, approximately 30 to 35 minutes per pound. Fresh ham, when done, should reach an internal temperature of 175 degrees on a meat thermometer.

While the ham is baking, prepare the glaze. One hour before the ham is done, remove it from the oven; cut away the rind with a sharp knife or kitchen shears. Score the fat diagonally ⅛-inch deep, to create a diamond pattern. Coat the roast with the mustard glaze and return it to the oven for the additional hour. When done, remove to a warm platter or carving board; discard the onion slices. Serve with Rosemary Mustard Sauce (page 198).

Serves eight to ten.

GLAZE

½ cup Dijon mustard
2 tablespoons dry sherry
2 tablespoons vegetable oil

In a small bowl whisk together all the ingredients.
Makes approximately ½ cup.

• Pork Chops in
Vinegar and Mustard •

8 center-cut pork chops,
½-inch thick, well
trimmed
Salt and freshly ground
black pepper to taste
½ cup flour
4 tablespoons olive oil
1 small onion, finely
chopped
1 cup finely chopped
mushrooms
3 tablespoons red wine
vinegar

1 cup beef stock
4 sprigs fresh rosemary
leaves or 1 teaspoon
dried rosemary leaves
2 tablespoons Dijon
mustard with green
peppercorns
2 tablespoons capers,
drained
Chopped fresh parsley

Preheat oven to 350 degrees.

Season the chops with salt and pepper and lightly coat
them with flour.

Heat the oil in a large skillet and brown the chops over
high heat for 5 minutes on each side. Remove them to a
shallow baking pan large enough to hold the chops in one
layer.

Pour off all but 2 tablespoons of the fat from the skillet
and sauté the onion and mushrooms briefly over medium
heat. Add the vinegar, stock and rosemary. Raise the heat
to high and bring the liquid to a boil. Scrape up all the
browned particles from the pan with a wooden spoon while
cooking for 1 minute. Remove the pan from the heat and
swirl in the mustard.

Pour the sauce over the chops and bake for 20 minutes.
Sprinkle with the capers and parsley and serve.

Serves four.

• Pork Medallions in
Tomato Mustard Sauce •

1½ pounds pork tenderloin
Salt and freshly ground
    black pepper to taste
2 tablespoons olive oil

1 tablespoon white mustard
    seeds
Tomato Mustard Sauce

Slice the tenderloin into medallions ¼-inch thick; trim off and discard fat. Season pork with salt and pepper.

Heat the oil in a large skillet. Sauté the meat over medium high heat for 5 minutes, add the mustard seeds to the pan, and continue cooking for an additional 5 minutes, turning medallions to brown all sides.

Add the tomato mustard sauce to the pan, mix to combine with the meat, lower heat to medium, and cook 5 minutes longer. Serve immediately.

Serves four.

TOMATO MUSTARD SAUCE

2 tablespoons olive oil
1 small onion, coarsely
    chopped
1 clove garlic, finely
    minced
2 cups canned Italian plum
    tomatoes, drained and
    coarsely chopped

1 teaspoon dried basil or 2
    tablespoons chopped
    fresh basil leaves
Salt and freshly ground
    black pepper to taste
1 tablespoon Dijon mustard

Heat the oil in a small skillet. Add the onion and garlic and cook for several minutes over medium heat until wilted. Add the tomatoes, basil, salt and pepper, and cook for 10 minutes longer. Remove the pan from the heat and stir in the mustard.

Makes 1½ cups.

• Pork Chops Parmesan •

8 center-cut pork chops,
½-inch thick
Salt and white pepper to
taste
2 tablespoons Dijon
mustard
Juice of 1 lemon
2 cloves garlic, crushed

½ cup olive oil
1½ cups fresh bread
crumbs
½ cup freshly grated
Parmesan cheese
3 tablespoons chopped
fresh parsley

Season the pork chops with salt and pepper.

In a small bowl whisk together the mustard, lemon juice, and garlic. Gradually whisk in the oil.

Place the pork chops in a dish large enough to hold them in one layer. Pour the marinade over them and turn them to coat all sides. Marinate for 2 hours at room temperature, turning frequently and basting with the marinade.

Preheat oven to 350 degrees.

Mix together the bread crumbs, cheese, and parsley, and have ready on a large sheet of waxed paper. Dredge the chops well on both sides with the mixture. Place them in one layer in a large shallow baking dish and bake for 50 minutes.

Serves four.

• About ¼ cup of Tomato Herb Mustard (page 76) added to stew gravy, especially lamb, provides extra body and extraordinary flavor.

• Make French Toast adding Dijon mustard to taste to the egg-milk mixture. Use toast as a base for tender slices of veal scaloppine with lemon sauce or for sliced steak. (Or don't add the mustard to the batter and use thin slices of Mustard Beer Bread [page 212] instead of white bread.)

• Stuffed Pork Chops in Cider •

4 center-cut pork chops,
  1 inch thick
1 cup fresh bread crumbs
1 clove garlic, crushed
2 tablespoons chopped
  fresh parsley
1 teaspoon dried, crumbled
  sage
Salt and freshly ground
  black pepper to taste
3 tablespoons heavy cream

1 teaspoon plus 2 table-
  spoons Dijon mustard
2 tablespoons olive oil
1 cup sweet apple cider
1 large McIntosh apple,
  peeled, cored, diced in
  small pieces
½ cup sour cream
Chopped fresh parsley

Preheat oven to 350 degrees.

Have the butcher cut a pocket in the side of each chop for stuffing, or do it yourself. Make a slash 3 inches long in the side of each chop with a sharp knife, and cut into the chop about 3 inches.

In a small bowl mix together the bread crumbs, garlic, parsley, sage, salt, pepper, heavy cream, and one teaspoon of mustard. Divide the stuffing into four portions and insert well into the pocket of each chop. Season the chops lightly with salt and pepper.

Heat the oil in a large skillet and brown the chops over high heat for 5 minutes on each side. Remove them to a shallow baking pan large enough to hold them in one layer.

Pour off all the fat from the skillet, add the cider, and boil for 1 minute over high heat, using a wooden spoon to scrape up all the browned particles from the skillet. Pour the sauce over the chops, scatter the diced apple around the chops, and bake for 30 minutes.

Remove the chops to a warm platter and keep warm. Add the sour cream and the remaining 2 tablespoons of mustard to the pan liquid and apple and cook over medium heat, stirring, for several minutes. Pour over the pork chops and sprinkle with parsley. Serve immediately.

Serves four.

• Herb-Coated Pork Loin •

4-pound boned center-cut pork loin (boned weight)
4 tablespoons Dijon mustard
2 tablespoons olive oil
4 to 5 large cloves garlic, crushed
1½ teaspoons coarse (kosher) salt
1 teaspoon freshly ground black pepper
1 teaspoon dried basil leaves

1 teaspoon dried rosemary leaves
½ teaspoon dried thyme leaves
1 teaspoon dried oregano
1 tablespoon dried parsley leaves
1 medium onion, thinly sliced
1 cup water
1 cup dry white wine

Preheat oven to 500 degrees.

In a small bowl whisk together the mustard and oil; add the garlic, salt, pepper, basil, rosemary, thyme, oregano, and parsley, and make a paste. Make several gashes in the meat with a sharp knife; rub the mixture into the gashes, over the surface of the meat, and into the seam.

Place the pork loin on top of the sliced onion in a roasting pan, add the water to the pan, and roast at high heat for 15 minutes. Lower the oven temperature to 350 degrees and pour the wine over the meat. Roast for a total of two hours, basting occasionally with the pan juices. Pork should reach an internal temperature of 175 degrees on a meat thermometer when done. Serve with the pan juices.

Serves six.

4-pound boned center-cut pork loin (boned weight)   1 tablespoon Dijon mustard
2 cups chicken stock   Apricot Glaze

Preheat oven to 500 degrees.

Place the pork loin in a roasting pan and roast at high heat for 15 minutes. Pour off the accumulated fat and lower oven temperature to 350 degrees. Continue to roast for an additional 45 minutes, and pour off fat once more. Add one cup of the chicken stock to the pan and spoon several tablespoons of the apricot glaze over the meat. Continue to roast for 1 hour longer or until the meat registers a temperature of 175 degrees on a meat thermometer. Baste with additional glaze several times more during the last hour, until the glaze is completely used.

Remove the roast to a warm platter and allow it to rest before slicing. To the pan juices, add the remaining cup of chicken stock and the tablespoon of mustard, whisk together, and cook for 1 minute over high heat. Serve the sauce separately.

Serves six.

APRICOT GLAZE
1 cup apricot preserves   1 teaspoon grated fresh
2 tablespoons dry sherry   ginger, optional
¼ cup Dijon mustard

In a small bowl whisk together the apricot preserves, sherry, mustard, and ginger (if desired).

Makes approximately 1 cup.

• Deviled Country-Style Spareribs •

8 country-style spareribs	¼ cup Dijon mustard
½ cup butter	2½ to 3 cups fresh bread
2 tablespoons red wine	crumbs
vinegar	

Melt the butter in a small saucepan; remove from heat, and whisk in the vinegar and mustard until smooth.

Coat the spareribs liberally with the mustard mixture. Have the bread crumbs ready on a sheet of waxed paper and roll the ribs in the bread crumbs, pressing with fingertips to make them adhere. Refrigerate for 1 hour.

Preheat oven to 375 degrees.

Place the spareribs on a rack set in a shallow roasting pan and bake for 1 hour. For a crisper crust, place under broiler for 2 to 3 minutes. Serve with Deviled Sauce I or II (pages 194 and 195).

Serves four.

• Mustard Spareribs with
Black Currant Preserves •

4 pounds spareribs	3 tablespoons dry sherry
¾ cup black currant	3 cloves garlic, crushed
preserves	¾ cup Dijon mustard

Preheat oven to 350 degrees.

Mix together in a small bowl the preserves, sherry, garlic, and mustard.

Trim the ribs of excess fat, leaving the racks of meat whole. Arrange the spareribs in one layer, meaty side up, on a rack in a large shallow roasting pan. Brush liberally with about one-half the mustard mixture. Bake in the middle of the oven for 45 minutes, brushing once with additional glaze. Turn the spareribs and coat the second side liberally with additional mixture, reserving some to brush once more during baking. Bake for an additional 45 minutes on the second side.

Remove the spareribs to a cutting board. With a sharp cleaver or knife, separate the meat into individual ribs. Have a warm serving platter ready.

Serves four.

• Choucroute Garnie •

3 pounds sauerkraut
4 slices bacon, ⅛-inch thick, in small pieces
1 medium onion, coarsely chopped
1 one-pound Kielbasa (Polish garlic sausage)
1 one-pound slice smoked ham steak
8 smoked loin pork chops
1 teaspoon peppercorns

2 cloves
1 teaspoon juniper berries
1 teaspoon white mustard seeds
1 bay leaf
3 cloves garlic, whole
1 cup chicken stock
1 cup dry white wine
¼ cup Dijon (or Dusseldorf) mustard

Place the sauerkraut in a colander and set aside to drain.

In a wide casserole or pot, sauté the bacon pieces over low heat for 2 minutes on each side until just softened. Remove the bacon with a slotted spoon and reserve. Add the onion to the pot and sauté in the bacon fat over low heat for 2 to 3 minutes until wilted. Return the bacon pieces to the pot. Place the drained sauerkraut in the pot; toss with the bacon pieces and onion. Arrange the sausage, ham steak, and pork chops over the sauerkraut. Place the peppercorns, cloves, juniper berries, mustard seeds, bay leaf, and garlic on a small square of cheesecloth and tie up securely with butchers' twine to make a small bag. Bury well into the sauerkraut.

In a bowl, whisk together the stock, wine, and mustard and add to the pot. Bring the liquid to a boil over high heat. Lower the heat and simmer, covered, for 1½ hours. Discard the cheesecloth bag. Transfer the sauerkraut and meats to a warm serving platter.

Serve with tiny boiled potatoes sprinkled with parsley and an assortment of mustards.

Serves six to eight.

• Spread thin slices of leftover roast beef trimmed of all fat and gristle with Horseradish Mustard (page 74), roll up jelly-roll fashion, and serve several as an appetizer or first course.

• Keep a small bowl or crock of Mustard Butter in the refrigerator ready to use as sauce on poached fish, chicken, even hamburger.

• Whisk mustard to taste into the pan drippings of any roast to enrich the taste.

• Smear mustard on chops, fillets of fish, chicken breasts, or anything you are coating with bread crumbs. They'll adhere better—and the addition makes the flavor sensational.

• Transform sliced, cooked leftover meats such as beef, lamb, or pork by smearing them with Dijon mustard (try a flavored one), dipping in bread crumbs, and broiling for several minutes until crusty.

• Split frankfurters down the middle lengthwise and fill with ball-park mustard *before* grilling or broiling.

• Spread Dijon mustard over steaks, chops, chicken, or fish before broiling or grilling.

ENTREES: POULTRY

• Chicken Breasts in Orange Sauce •

4 whole chicken breasts,
    skinned, boned, and
    halved
Salt and white pepper to
    taste
½ cup flour
2 tablespoons butter
2 tablespoons olive oil
1 cup chicken stock
½ cup fresh orange juice

1 tablespoon cornstarch
3 teaspoons dry mustard
½ teaspoon ground
    cinnamon
Dash of ground cloves
Grated rind of 1 orange
½ cup coarsely chopped
    almonds
1 orange, peeled and
    sectioned

Slice each halved chicken breast into 3 pieces
lengthwise. Season the chicken with salt and pepper and
dredge in the flour.

Melt the butter and oil in a large skillet and quickly sauté
the chicken pieces over high heat for several minutes on
each side until lightly browned. Remove them to a platter
and reserve skillet for later use.

In a small saucepan mix together the stock, juice,
cornstarch, dry mustard, cinnamon, cloves, and orange
rind, and cook over medium heat, whisking, until the sauce
thickens slightly. Keep warm over low heat.

Sauté the almonds in the reserved skillet for 1 minute
and return the chicken pieces to the pan.

Pour in the orange sauce and cook together on high heat,

---

scraping up all the browned particles from the pan with a wooden spoon. Lower heat to medium and cook for 10 minutes longer. Add the orange sections during the last 2 or 3 minutes of cooking.

Serves six to eight.

• Chicken Breasts with Sour Cream •

4 whole chicken breasts, skinned, boned, and halved
Salt and white pepper to taste
1 cup sour cream
2 tablespoons Dijon mustard with lemon
3 cups fresh bread crumbs
4 tablespoons butter
4 tablespoons vegetable oil

Place the halved chicken breasts between two sheets of waxed paper and pound flat with a metal meat pounder or the wide blade of a meat cleaver. Season the breasts with salt and pepper.

In a wide bowl mix together the sour cream and mustard. Have the bread crumbs ready on a sheet of waxed paper. Coat the chicken-breast halves, one at a time, with the sour cream-mustard mixture, then with the bread crumbs, pressing the crumbs onto the chicken with fingers so that coating adheres well.

Place the chicken on a large platter, cover with waxed paper, and refrigerate for several hours.

Melt the butter and oil in a large skillet and, when sizzling, add the chicken breasts, several at a time. Brown over medium heat, about 6 minutes on each side. Keep the browned breasts warm in a low oven while continuing to cook the remaining pieces.

Serves six to eight.

• Pecan Chicken Breasts •

4 whole chicken breasts,
skinned, boned, and
halved
Salt and white pepper to
taste
6 tablespoons Dijon
mustard
12 tablespoons butter,
melted

1 tablespoon lemon juice
1½ cups fresh bread
crumbs
1½ cups finely ground
pecans
4 tablespoons butter
4 tablespoons vegetable oil

Place the halved chicken breasts between two sheets of
waxed paper and pound flat with a metal meat pounder or
the wide blade of a meat cleaver. Season the breasts with
salt and pepper.

Place the mustard in a bowl and gradually whisk in the
melted butter. Add the lemon juice. Mix together the
bread crumbs and pecans and have ready on a sheet of
waxed paper. Dip the chicken breasts into the mustard
mixture to coat them on all sides, then into the bread
crumb-pecan mixture. Transfer the chicken breasts to a
large platter, cover with waxed paper, and refrigerate for
several hours.

Melt the butter and oil in a large skillet and, when
sizzling, add the chicken breasts, several at a time. If any of
the coating falls off the breasts, push it to the side of the
pan or remove. Brown over medium heat, about 6 minutes
on each side. Keep the browned breasts warm in a low oven
while continuing to cook the remaining pieces.

Serves six to eight.

• Chicken Kiev/Dijon •

1 recipe Mustard Butter
  (page 193)
4 whole chicken breasts,
  skinned, boned, and
  halved
Large bunch fresh dill,
  chopped

Salt and white pepper to
  taste
2 eggs
¼ cup flour
1 cup fresh bread crumbs
Vegetable oil for deep
  frying

Make the mustard butter. Shape into a stick and chill until firm.

Place the boned chicken breasts between 2 sheets of waxed paper and pound them flat. Season with salt and pepper and place a generous amount of dill on each.

Cut the stick of chilled butter in half lengthwise, then crosswise into quarters, giving you 8 pieces. Place one piece in the center of each breast. Fold in the long sides and roll the breast up, pushing and stretching it to completely encase the butter. Chill for 1 hour or until firm.

Beat the eggs in a bowl. Have the flour and bread crumbs set on a large sheet of waxed paper in two separate piles. Dredge each rolled breast in flour, then dip into the eggs, covering all surfaces, then roll in the bread crumbs. Using two forks makes this somewhat messy procedure less messy. Chill the breasts again, this time for several hours or even overnight.

Preheat oven to 400 degrees.

Heat the oil in a deep-fat fryer or a deep pot. It should register 360 degrees on a fat thermometer. Add the chicken, a few pieces at a time; do not crowd the pot. Fry until browned, about 5 minutes, Remove to paper towels to drain. When all the breasts are cooked and drained, transfer them to a baking pan and bake for 10 minutes.

Serves four.

• Deviled Mustard-Basil Chicken •

2 2½-pound frying
chickens, cut into
serving pieces
Salt and white pepper to
taste
¼ cup dry white wine
¾ cup Dijon mustard

¼ cup fresh basil leaves,
chopped, or 1 tablespoon
dried basil leaves
4 tablespoons butter
4 tablespoons vegetable oil
1 tablespoon lemon juice
2 cups fresh bread crumbs

Preheat broiler to high.

Rinse and dry the chicken pieces well, season with salt and pepper, and arrange skin-side down in a large baking pan.

In a small bowl combine the wine, mustard, and basil, and set aside.

Melt the butter in a small saucepan and stir in the oil and lemon juice. Spoon this mixture over the chicken and broil about 5 inches away from the heat, 10 minutes on each side. Baste several times, watching chicken so as not to burn. Remove from the oven and reserve the basting fat and juices.

Have bread crumbs ready on a sheet of waxed paper. Coat the chicken pieces thoroughly with the mustard mixture and roll in the crumbs, patting them to adhere well. Arrange the chicken on a rack in a broiling pan and dribble the reserved fat and juices over them.

Reduce broiler heat to low; broil again for 10 minutes on each side until browned.

Serves four.

NOTE: Substitute chicken parts such as all legs, wings, thighs, or breasts, instead of whole cut-up chicken.

• Savory Chicken Fricassee •

4-pound roasting chicken, cut into serving pieces
2 teaspoons salt
1 teaspoon freshly ground black pepper
1 teaspoon paprika
1 teaspoon dry mustard
4 tablespoons butter
2 tablespoons vegetable oil
1 cup dry white wine
3 cups chicken stock
1 bay leaf, split in half
3 peppercorns
Several sprigs of fresh parsley
2 carrots, scraped, cut crosswise in 3
1 small onion, stuck with 2 cloves
1 celery stalk, including leafy top, cut crosswise in 2
2 egg yolks
1 cup heavy cream
3 tablespoons Dijon mustard
1 tablespoon lemon juice

Wash the chicken pieces and dry well with paper towels. Mix together the salt, pepper, paprika, and dry mustard, and rub the mixture into the chicken pieces.

In a large, heavy Dutch oven or casserole, heat the butter and oil and, when sizzling, add as many chicken pieces as the pot will hold in one layer. Brown the chicken, about 3 minutes on each side. Remove to a platter and continue to brown the rest of the pieces. When all the pieces have been browned, return them to the casserole. Add the wine, chicken stock, bay leaf, peppercorns, parsley, carrots, onion, and celery. Bring the liquid to a boil over high heat, lower heat, and simmer, covered, for 1 hour or until the chicken is tender. Remove the chicken to a platter and strain the cooking liquid. Pour back into the casserole. Reserve the carrots and slice into thin rounds.

In a small bowl whisk together the egg yolks, heavy cream, prepared mustard, and lemon juice.

Bring the liquid in the casserole to a boil over high heat; add ½ cup to the cream mixture, whisking briskly to prevent curdling. Pour into the casserole, continue to stir, lower the heat to medium, and cook for 5 minutes, or until slightly thickened. Return the chicken pieces and the sliced carrots to the casserole and heat through; do not allow to boil. Serve with Mustard Dumplings (page 217).

Serves four.

• Chicken Parmesan •

2 2½ pound frying
chickens, cut into
serving pieces
Salt and white pepper to
taste
4 tablespoons Dijon
mustard
Juice of 2 lemons
4 cloves garlic, crushed

1 cup olive oil
1 tablespoon dried basil
leaves
2 cups fresh bread crumbs
¾ cup freshly grated
Parmesan cheese
¼ cup chopped fresh
parsley

Wash and dry the chicken pieces well. Season with salt and pepper.

In a small bowl whisk together the mustard, lemon juice, and garlic. Whisk in the oil gradually and mix in the basil leaves.

Place the chicken pieces in a large deep bowl and cover with the marinade. Marinate for 2 hours at room temperature, turning occasionally to coat all surfaces of the chicken.

Mix together the bread crumbs, cheese, and parsley, and have ready on a large sheet of waxed paper.

Preheat oven to 400 degrees.

Dredge the chicken on all sides in the bread-crumb mixture and arrange in a shallow baking pan large enough to hold the pieces in one layer. Bake for 45 minutes until crusty and browned.

Serves four.

• Mustard Tarragon Chicken •

3½-pound chicken, cut
  into serving pieces
Salt and white pepper to
  taste
½ cup flour
2 tablespoons butter
2 tablespoons oil
½ cup Dijon mustard with
  tarragon

1 medium onion, coarsely
  chopped
¼ pound mushrooms,
  coarsely chopped
⅓ cup dry sherry
⅓ cup chicken stock
1 cup heavy cream

Preheat oven to 350 degrees.

Wash the chicken pieces and dry with paper towels. Sprinkle the pieces with salt and pepper and dredge in flour to coat all sides.

In a large skillet heat the butter and oil and add the chicken, skin side down. Brown as many pieces as the skillet will hold without crowding, over medium-high heat, 5 minutes on each side. As they are done, transfer the chicken pieces, skin side up, to a large baking dish. Continue to brown the remaining pieces. When all the chicken pieces are arranged in baking dish, coat the skin thickly with the mustard.

To the skillet add the onion and sauté over medium heat, about 5 minutes, until transparent. Add the mushrooms; cook for 1 minute longer. Pour in the sherry and stock, raise the heat to high, and scrape all browned particles from the pan with a wooden spoon. Remove the pan from the heat; stir in the heavy cream. Return to low heat and cook for 5 minutes, being careful not to boil the cream. Pour the sauce over the chicken and bake for 30 minutes.

Serves four.

• Mustard Tarragon Rabbit •

Follow the directions for mustard-coated chicken in the preceding recipe, substituting rabbit for the chicken.

• Chicken Livers in Mustard Cream •

1½ pounds chicken livers
½ cup flour
Salt and white pepper to taste
2 egg yolks
1 cup heavy cream
3 tablespoons Dijon grainy mustard

3 tablespoons butter
3 tablespoons vegetable oil
2 medium onions, coarsely chopped
3 tablespoons cognac
2 tablespoons chopped fresh parsley

Rinse the livers, trim and discard any fat, pat dry. Put the flour on a sheet of waxed paper, dredge the livers in the flour, and season lightly with salt and pepper.

In a small bowl beat the egg yolks with the heavy cream and mustard and reserve.

Heat the butter and oil in a large skillet and, when hot, add the onions. Brown them lightly over medium heat for 5 minutes, mixing with a wooden spoon. Add the chicken livers, turn the heat to high, and sauté for another 5 minutes, or until liver looses its pinkness.

Pour in the cognac, set aflame, and continue cooking, shaking the handle of the pan until the flame dies. Scrape up all the browned particles clinging to the pan using a wooden spoon.

Stir in the cream mixture and cook for 3 minutes, just until the sauce thickens. Do not boil.

Sprinkle with the parsley and serve.

Serves four.

NOTE: For a variation try this recipe with ½-inch-thick calves' liver cut in long strips. Proceed as above.

• Chicken Salad with Mustard Mayonnaise •

3 pounds chicken breasts
  with ribs attached
1 carrot, scraped, cut
  crosswise in 2
1 celery stalk, including
  leafy top, cut crosswise
  in 2
1 small onion stuck with 2
  cloves
1 bay leaf, split in half
Several sprigs of fresh
  parsley
1 clove garlic
1 14-ounce can whole
  artichoke hearts,
  drained, or 1 9-ounce

package frozen, cooked
  and cooled
1 medium onion, coarsely
  chopped
3 tablespoons snipped fresh
  dill
Salt and freshly ground
  black pepper to taste
1½ cups Mustard
  Mayonnaise (page 192)
½ pound fresh mushrooms,
  sliced
Bunch of watercress
Fresh dill sprigs

Place the chicken breasts in a saucepan, cover with cold water, and add the carrot, celery, small onion stuck with cloves, bay leaf, parsley, and garlic. Bring the liquid to a boil over high heat, lower the heat, and simmer, covered, for 35 minutes. Remove the chicken breasts from the liquid and allow to cool. Strain and freeze the stock for future use.

When the breasts are cool enough to handle, remove and discard the skin and bones. Dice the chicken meat into large cubes and place in a mixing bowl. Quarter the artichoke hearts and add to the chicken together with the chopped onion, dill, salt, pepper, and Mustard Mayonnaise. Toss to coat all the ingredients thoroughly. Chill for several hours before serving.

Just before serving, fold in the sliced fresh mushrooms. Transfer the salad to a large serving bowl. Arrange watercress around the edge of the salad; sprinkle salad with additional dill.

Serves six.

• Duck with Green Peppercorn Mustard •

5-pound duckling
Rind of 3 navel oranges,
   cut into julienne strips 2
   inches in length
Half a lemon
Salt and white pepper to
   taste
1 cup water

½ cup dry white wine
3 tablespoons Madeira wine
1 tablespoon cornstarch
2 tablespoons Dijon
   mustard with green
   peppercorns
Glaze-recipe follows
Giblet Sauce-recipe follows

Place the orange rind strips in one quart of water and simmer over medium heat for 15 minutes. Drain and set aside on paper towels to dry.

Make glaze (recipe follows) and set aside.

Preheat oven to 350 degrees.

Remove the giblets and neck from the duck and reserve for giblet sauce. Wash the bird, then dry well with paper towels, both inside and out. Pull out and discard the excess fat from the cavity openings and rub the duck inside and out with the cut side of the lemon half, squeezing out the juice onto and into the duck. Season inside and out with salt and pepper. Pierce the entire surface of the skin with a fork. Place a small handful of the strips of orange rind in the cavity, reserving the rest. Fold the wings under the back and tie the legs together with butchers' twine. Place the duck on its side on a rack in a roasting pan.

Spoon a small amount of the glaze over the duck and add the cup of water and ½ cup of white wine to the pan. Roast, basting every 15 minutes with additional glaze, ½ hour on the first side, then ½ hour on the second side. Place breast up for the balance of cooking time, 1½ hours longer. It will turn golden brown. While roasting, pierce the skin of the duck frequently with a fork and press down to allow the fat to run out. This will make the skin crisp. While the duck is roasting, prepare Giblet Sauce (recipe follows).

When the duck is done, remove it to a warm serving platter; remove and discard twine. Pour off the fat from the roasting pan; add the strained giblet sauce to the pan juices together with the Madeira. Boil over high heat for 1 minute. Place the cornstarch in a small bowl, remove two tablespoons of the liquid from the pan, combine it with the cornstarch, and whisk until smooth. Pour mixture back into the pan and cook over medium heat for 5 minutes, stirring, until sauce thickens slightly. Remove the pan from the heat, whisk in the mustard, and add the reserved orange rind. Quarter the duck, place on individual plates, and coat generously with sauce. Pass the additional sauce separately.

Serves four.

GLAZE

1 cup orange marmalade	2 teaspoons dry mustard
½ cup dry white wine	1 teaspoon ground ginger
2 tablespoons soy sauce	1 clove garlic, crushed

Combine all the ingredients in a small saucepan and cook over low heat for 5 minutes.

Makes 1½ cups.

GIBLET SAUCE

Giblets and neck from duck	1 carrot, scraped, cut
1 cup chicken stock	crosswise in 3
½ cup dry white wine	1 small onion stuck with
1 teaspoon salt	2 cloves
Freshly ground black	Several sprigs of fresh
pepper to taste	parsley

Rinse the giblets and neck and place in a small saucepan with the remaining ingredients. Bring to a boil over high heat, skim off any scum rising to the surface, turn heat to low, and simmer, covered, for 1 hour. Strain the stock and reserve.

Makes approximately 1½ cups.

• Whisk Dijon mustard into buttermilk, marinate chicken pieces in the mixture, dip them in flour, and fry in deep fat for a variation on southern fried chicken.

• Before broiling or grilling chicken, meat, fish, or shrimp, brush with melted Mustard Butter (page 193).

• Lightly coat cold sliced chicken arranged on a platter with mayonnaise mixed with green-peppercorn Dijon mustard to taste, and thinned with a little cream or half-and-half. Sprinkle with chopped parsley or mustard sprouts.

• Add a tablespoon or two of an appropriately flavored Dijon mustard to a stuffing for turkey or chicken.

• To give a very special flavor to roast chicken, turkey, cornish hen, or squab, make a paste of 2 tablespoons of softened butter, 1 tablespoon of Dijon mustard, 1 crushed garlic clove, and a tablespoon of dried rosemary leaves. Smear generously over entire surface of bird; place on its side on a rack and roast. When done, remove bird to heated platter, add Giblet Sauce (page 147) to pan juices, and bring to a boil for one minute. Serve sauce separately.

• Mustard is the proper matchmaker to marry some of those odd-sounding *nouvelle cuisine* combinations of fruits with fish or meat. It makes two or more disparate personalities compatible. If lobster and blueberries or duck livers and kiwi fruit must be combined, mustard in a light cream sauce can give them togetherness.

ENTREES: FISH AND SHELLFISH

• Stuffed Red Snapper Creole •

1 4-pound red snapper	½ teaspoon dried basil leaves
Salt and white pepper to taste	¼ teaspoon dried thyme leaves
2 tablespoons butter	½ bay leaf
1 small onion, coarsely chopped	1 tablespoon chopped fresh parsley
1 clove garlic, finely minced	1 teaspoon grated lemon rind
1 celery stalk, coarsely chopped	Dash of Tabasco
1 small green pepper, coarsely chopped	2 tablespoons Creole mustard
1 cup canned Italian plum tomatoes, drained and coarsely chopped	4 tablespoons melted butter
	1 cup dry white wine

Ask at the fish market to have head removed from the fish, leaving tail intact. Have the fish split open, book-style, and bones removed.

Preheat oven to 350 degrees.

Place the fish in a large oval buttered baking dish and liberally season with the salt and pepper inside and out.

Melt the butter in a skillet and add the onion, garlic, celery, and green pepper. Cook over medium heat for 3 minutes, stirring. Add the tomatoes, basil, thyme, bay leaf, parsley, lemon rind, and Tabasco, and cook for 5 minutes longer. Stuff the fish with the vegetable mixture.

Place the mustard in a small bowl. Gradually whisk in the melted butter until creamy. Add the wine, continuing to whisk until thoroughly mixed. Pour this mixture over the stuffed fish. Bake for 40 minutes, basting occasionally with the pan juices.

Serves four.

• Baked Salmon Loaf •

2 15½-ounce cans salmon (approximately 4 cups), or 4 cups leftover cooked salmon
1 cup fresh white bread crumbs
3 tablespoons snipped fresh dill
3 tablespoons Dijon mustard with lemon
1 medium onion, coarsely grated
½ teaspoon white pepper
¼ cup sour cream
2 eggs, well beaten

Preheat oven to 375 degrees.

Drain the canned salmon well. Place in a large mixing bowl along with the remaining ingredients. Mix thoroughly.

Turn the salmon mixture into a well-buttered 8½ × 4½ × 2½-inch loaf pan. Bake for 45 minutes. Cool in the pan for 5 minutes before turning out onto a serving platter. Serve hot with Mustard Hollandaise (page 169) or cold with Watercress Sauce (page 191).

Serves six.

• Poached Salmon in Egg Mustard Sauce •

4 salmon steaks, ½-inch
   thick
2 cups dry white wine
1 small onion, halved
2 tablespoons tarragon
   vinegar
1 teaspoon salt

3 peppercorns
1 celery stalk, cut crosswise
   in 2
Several sprigs of parsley
½ bay leaf
Egg Mustard Sauce

Place the salmon in a deep skillet large enough to hold the salmon steaks in one layer. Add the remaining ingredients except mustard sauce. Bring the liquid to a boil over high heat, lower the heat, and simmer, covered, for about 10 minutes or until the salmon flakes easily with a fork. Gently remove the salmon to a warm serving platter and keep warm while preparing the Egg Mustard sauce. Strain and reserve one cup of the poaching liquid for the sauce.

Coat the salmon steaks with the sauce or pass it separately.

Serves four.

EGG MUSTARD SAUCE

2 tablespoons butter
2 tablespoons flour
1 cup poaching liquid from
   salmon*
1 cup heavy cream
¼ cup Dijon mustard
1 tablespoon lemon juice

2 tablespoons snipped fresh
   dill
2 hard-cooked eggs,
   coarsely chopped
Salt and white pepper to
   taste

Melt the butter in a saucepan, whisk in the flour, and cook over low heat for 1 minute. Add the strained poaching liquid and continue to whisk, cooking for 2 to 3 minutes

---

*To serve with baked fish or boiled shrimp, substitute bottled clam juice for the poaching liquid. For vegetables or poached chicken, substitute chicken stock for the poaching liquid.

longer, until slightly thickened. Beat the heavy cream and mustard in a small bowl and add gradually, whisking. Simmer for 5 minutes. Remove the pan from the heat. Stir in the lemon juice, dill, and hard-cooked eggs. Add salt and pepper to taste.

Serve this sauce with any poached or baked fish; also good on hot, boiled shrimp, cooked vegetables, or poached chicken.

Makes approximately 2 cups.

• Scallops in Mustard Cream •

1½ pounds bay scallops
½ cup flour
2 tablespoons butter
2 tablespoons vegetable oil
2 shallots, finely chopped
3 tablespoons dry sherry
1 cup heavy cream

3 tablespoons Dijon
   mustard with green
   peppercorns
Salt and freshly ground
   black pepper to taste
2 tablespoons chopped
   fresh parsley

Rinse the scallops under cold running water. If bay scallops are unavailable, use quartered sea scallops. Dry on paper towels, then dredge them in the flour. Set aside.

Melt the butter and oil in a large skillet and add the shallots. Cook for 1 minute over medium heat, add the scallops, raise the heat to high, and quickly sauté for several minutes, shaking the pan, until they are golden. Reduce the heat to medium, add the sherry, and cook until the liquid evaporates.

In a small bowl whisk together the cream, mustard, salt, and pepper, and pour into the pan. Mix well to coat the scallops and heat through for 2 minutes. Do not allow to boil. Sprinkle with parsley and serve immediately.

Serves four.

• Sweet-and-Sour Shrimp •

1½ pounds medium-sized
  shrimp
½ cup dried apricots, diced
Boiling water
1 large ripe tomato
½ cup rice wine vinegar, or
  white vinegar
4 teaspoons dry mustard
1 tablespoon cornstarch
¼ cup sugar

2 tablespoons soy sauce
½ cup dry sherry
3 tablespoons vegetable oil
1 large onion, halved,
  thinly sliced
1 large green bell pepper,
  seeded, cored, cut into
  ½-inch strips
3 scallions, greens
  included, sliced

Peel and devein the shrimp; rinse and pat dry with paper towels and set aside. Place the apricots in a small bowl, cover with boiling water, and allow to sit for 10 minutes. Drain and set aside. Place the tomato in a small bowl, cover with boiling water, and allow to sit for 1 minute. Drain and slip off skin. Cut into eighths and set aside.

In a small bowl whisk the vinegar with the dry mustard and cornstarch until dissolved; add the sugar, soy sauce, and sherry, and whisk thoroughly.

Heat the oil in a large skillet, add the onion, and sauté over medium heat for 1 minute. Add the green pepper and continue cooking for 2 to 3 minutes longer. Do not overcook; the green pepper should remain crisp. Add the shrimp, apricots, and tomato, and continue to cook, stirring to mix ingredients together, for about 3 minutes or until the shrimp turn pink. Pour the mustard mixture into the skillet, raise the heat to medium high, and cook for several minutes longer until the sauce is thickened. Remove the pan from the heat, sprinkle with the scallions, and serve immediately.

Serves four.

• Broiled Scampi in
Mustard Dill Marinade •

1½ pounds large shrimp
Mustard Dill Marinade

Peel the shrimp, leaving the tail segment on. Butterfly them by cutting with a sharp knife along the back to split them almost in two. Be careful not to cut completely through. Remove any veins, rinse thoroughly, lay them out flat on paper towels, and pat dry.

Place the shrimp in a bowl, cover with the marinade, and toss to coat them well. Refrigerate and marinate for at least 2 hours before broiling. Mix occasionally. Broil in the marinade for 8 to 10 minutes under a preheated broiler set on high.

Serves four.

MUSTARD DILL MARINADE

¼ cup Dijon mustard with lemon
2 cloves garlic, crushed
1 teaspoon soy sauce
Pinch of cayenne pepper (optional)
1 cup olive oil
½ cup snipped fresh dill

Place the mustard, garlic, soy sauce, and cayenne pepper in a small bowl. Whisk together and slowly add the oil, whisking until the marinade is creamy. Fold in the dill.

Makes approximately 1½ cups.

NOTE: Use the marinade when broiling any fish or shellfish.

• Steamed Mussels in Mustard Broth •

5 pounds mussels
4 tablespoons butter
1 large onion, coarsely
  chopped
2 celery stalks, leafy top
  included, coarsely
  chopped
1 bay leaf, split in half
2 cloves
3 cloves garlic, finely
  minced

1 teaspoon dried thyme
  leaves
1½ cups dry white wine
3 tablespoons Dijon
  mustard
Salt and freshly ground
  black pepper to taste
Chopped fresh parsley

Scrub the mussels thoroughly, pull off beards, and rinse in several changes of cold water.

Melt the butter in a large deep skillet or fish poacher and add the onion, celery, bay leaf, cloves, garlic, and thyme, and sauté for 5 minutes over medium heat until the vegetables are softened but not browned. Add the wine and the mustard, whisking until blended; raise the heat to high and bring the liquid to a boil.

Add the mussels, cover the pot, and cook over medium heat for about 10 minutes or until the shells open. Shake the pot frequently or stir the mussels with a wooden spoon during the cooking. When done, transfer the mussels with a slotted spoon to a large warm serving bowl or individual warm soup bowls. Discard any unopened mussels. Add salt and pepper to the broth and spoon over the mussels. Sprinkle with parsley.

Serves four.

• Mussels in Mustard Cream Broth •

Cook the mussels as in previous recipe. When they are done and transferred to serving bowls, add 1 cup of heavy cream to the cooking liquid. Raise the heat to high and cook for 1 minute to heat through. Do not boil. Spoon the liquid over the mussels and sprinkle with parsley.

Substitute clams for the mussels in this or the preceding recipes, if you like.

• Deviled Soft-Shelled Crabs •

8 to 12 soft-shelled crabs (allow 2 to 3 per person, depending upon size)	½ cup flour 1½ cups fresh bread crumbs
3 eggs	½ cup butter
3 tablespoons Dijon mustard with lemon	Lemon wedges Chopped fresh parsley

Have the soft-shelled crabs cleaned and prepared for cooking at the fish market.

In a small bowl beat the eggs and whisk in the mustard thoroughly. Have the flour and bread crumbs ready on a large sheet of waxed paper.

Rinse the crabs under cold running water and pat dry with paper towels. Dredge them in the flour, dip into the egg mixture, and coat thoroughly with the bread crumbs. Place in one layer on a large platter, cover with waxed paper, and refrigerate for 1 hour.

Melt the butter in a large skillet; sauté the crabs over medium-high heat 5 minutes on each side, until golden brown. If your pan will not hold the crabs in one layer, do them in two or three batches and keep in a warm oven.

Transfer the crabs to a warm serving platter, pour the pan juices over them, and serve with lemon wedges. Sprinkle with chopped parsley.

Serves four.

- Dot clams on the half shell with Mustard Butter (page 193), sprinkle with bread crumbs, and broil; serve hot as an appetizer.

- The fresh roe of fish other than shad is economical and becomes a savory delicacy when sautéed in Mustard Butter (page 193) and served with lots of fresh lemon and parsley.

- Add a couple of tablespoons of Dijon mustard to a fish stew like bouillabaisse or cioppino—sacriligious to purists, exquisitely delicious to everyone else.

- Cool the Mussels in Mustard Cream Broth (page 156), shell the mussels, return to cream broth, and serve as sauce for cooked and *cooled* linguini. A surprisingly refreshing warm-weather supper.

- Serve Horseradish Mustard (page 74) instead of the ubiquitous cocktail sauce with raw shellfish or cooked shrimp.

- Cold seafood salad takes on a peppery wallop with mustard vinaigrette made with dry mustard or mustard oil substituted for half the olive oil.

- Add a tablespoon or two of lemon-flavored Dijon mustard to fish-poaching liquid before turning it into aspic.

- Add Dijon or Dusseldorf mustard to the batter for quenelles, codfish cakes, and potato puffs to give them your own personal flavor signature.

EGGS, CHEESE, AND PASTA

• Swiss Onion-Cheese Tart •

½ recipe, Short-Pastry
  Dough (page 214)
2 tablespoons Dijon
  mustard
½ pound cheese, coarsely
  grated (Swiss, Gruyère,
  Cheddar, or a mixture)
1 tablespoon flour
1 large onion, halved,
  thinly sliced

3 eggs
1 cup light cream
¼ teaspoon ground nutmeg
½ teaspoon salt
White pepper to taste
3 tablespoons freshly grated
  Parmesan cheese

Line a 9-inch quiche or pie pan with the pastry; prick the bottom and sides with a sharp fork. Chill for 30 minutes.

Preheat oven to 400 degrees.

Line the pie pan with a sheet of waxed paper, fill with a cup of dried beans or uncooked rice, and bake for 5 minutes, until the crust is set. Remove the pie pan from the oven, carefully remove the rice and waxed paper, and discard. Allow the crust to cool slightly.

Spread the bottom and sides of the partially baked crust with the mustard. In a bowl mix the grated Swiss cheese with the flour and spread evenly over the mustard. Arrange the sliced onion on top in an overlapping pattern.

Beat the eggs, cream, nutmeg, salt, and pepper in a small bowl. Pour over the onions and cheese. Sprinkle with the

Parmesan cheese, place the filled pastry shell on a baking sheet, and bake for 15 minutes. Reduce the oven heat to 325 degrees and bake for 30 minutes longer or until the custard is firm in the center.

Serves four to six.

NOTE: Baked tart may be frozen for up to 2 months, well-wrapped in freezer paper or plastic. To reheat, place the frozen tart in a preheated 350-degree oven and bake for 50 minutes.

• Eggs Scrambled in Mustard Butter •

6 eggs	6 tablespoons Mustard
½ cup heavy cream	Butter (page 193)
Salt and freshly ground	2 tablespoons chopped
black pepper to taste	chives or scallions

In a bowl beat the eggs lightly with the cream, salt, and pepper.

Heat 3 tablespoons of the mustard butter in a skillet, and when sizzling, add the eggs. Cook over low heat. Stir with a wooden spoon, making long strokes across the pan, always from the sides in toward the center. When the eggs are still soft but beginning to cook, add the remaining 3 tablespoons of mustard butter bit by bit, stirring gently into the eggs. Remove from the heat before they become too firm.

Serve immediately, sprinkled with chives or scallions. For an elegant luncheon or supper dish, serve with small bowls of caviar and sour cream.

Serves four.

• Poached Eggs with Ham
in Mustard Sauce •

4 slices ham
2 tablespoons butter
4 English muffin halves,
  toasted
4 eggs, at room temperature
Cold water
½ teaspoon salt
1 teaspoon white vinegar

1 tablespoon flour
½ cup water (from
  poaching liquid)
½ cup milk
1 tablespoon Dijon mustard
3 or 4 tablespoons chopped
  chives

Sauté the ham briefly in 1 tablespoon of the butter. Place one slice on each half of the toasted English muffins and keep warm in a low oven while poaching the eggs.

Poach the eggs in a shallow skillet. Fill with cold water to within ¾-inch from the rim, add the salt and vinegar, and bring the liquid to a boil over high heat. Lower the heat to medium and allow the bubbles to subside. Break the eggs, one at a time, into a small saucer and slip each gently into the water. Simmer for about 2 or 3 minutes. While cooking, spoon some of the liquid over the tops of the eggs. When the whites are firm, remove the eggs with a slotted spoon and drain on paper towels. Remove the muffin halves from the oven, arrange on individual plates, top each one with an egg, and keep warm.

Melt the remaining tablespoon of butter in a small saucepan, add the flour, and whisk together for 1 minute over low heat, until smooth. Add ½ cup water from the poached eggs and the milk, raise the heat to medium, and whisk until slightly thickened and smooth. Remove from the heat and whisk in the mustard. Pour the sauce over the eggs, sprinkle with chives, and serve immediately.

Serves two or four.

• Swedish Mustard Eggs •

2 tablespoons butter
2 tablespoons flour
1 cup milk
3 tablespoons spicy brown
  mustard
2 tablespoons snipped fresh
  dill

8 hard-cooked eggs
¼ cup herring fillets in
  wine sauce, drained,
  finely diced

Melt the butter in a small saucepan. Add the flour and whisk together over medium heat. Gradually add the milk, continuing to whisk until the sauce thickens. Remove the pan from the heat and stir in the mustard and dill.

Halve the eggs lengthwise, place the yolks in a small bowl, and mash with a fork. Mix the yolks with the herring and about ¼ cup of the mustard sauce. Mound this mixture into the egg whites and place in a baking dish. Spoon the remaining sauce over the eggs. Bake for 6 to 8 minutes until hot.

Serves eight.

• Welsh Rabbit •

4 slices home-style
  sandwich bread, toasted
2 tablespoons butter
½ pound sharp Cheddar
  cheese, coarsely grated
1 tablespoon flour
¼ cup beer

1 teaspoon Worcestershire
  sauce
1 teaspoon dry mustard
1 tablespoon Dijon mustard
Pinch of cayenne pepper
1 egg

Preheat broiler to high.

Halve the toast slices diagonally and arrange in 2 or 4 shallow individual baking dishes.

Melt the butter in a small saucepan over low heat, add the cheese and flour, and allow to cook slowly, stirring occasionally. Stir in the beer, Worcestershire sauce, dry mustard, prepared mustard, and cayenne pepper. Continue to stir until the mixture is smooth.

Beat the egg in a small bowl. Remove the cheese mixture from the heat and stir in the egg. Pour the cheese mixture over the toast; place the dishes under the broiler, about 3 inches away from the heat. Broil for 1 minute to brown lightly. Serve immediately.

Serves two or four.

• Soufflé Roll •

Melted butter and flour for
   the pan
4 tablespoons butter
½ cup flour
Salt and white pepper to
   taste

2 cups milk
5 eggs, separated
2 tablespoons Dijon
   mustard

Preheat oven to 400 degrees.

Butter a 15½ × 10½ × 1-inch jelly-roll pan, line with waxed paper, butter the waxed paper well, and dust lightly with flour.

Melt the butter in a saucepan over low heat; whisk in the flour, salt, and pepper. Gradually whisk in the milk and bring to a boil, stirring. Cook for 1 minute, until slightly thickened.

Beat the egg yolks in a small bowl; add a little of the hot mixture, stirring. Pour the egg-yolk mixture into the saucepan and cook over medium heat for 1 minute longer, stirring. Do not allow the sauce to boil. Remove the pan from the heat, whisk in the mustard, and set aside to cool.

Beat the egg whites until stiff but not dry. Fold into the cooled sauce. Pour into the prepared jelly-roll pan and bake for 30 minutes, until puffed and browned. Turn out the soufflé immediately, upside-down, onto a fresh sheet of waxed paper. Carefully remove the waxed paper covering it. Spread with the warm filling and roll, starting at one of the long sides, lifting the fresh waxed paper to help you roll it.

The roll can be served immediately or reheated on an unbuttered cookie sheet for 15 to 20 minutes in a preheated 350-degree oven.

Serves six.

FILLING

2 tablespoons butter
½ pound sweet Italian sausage meat
1 medium onion, coarsely chopped
¼ pound mushrooms, coarsely chopped
1 10-ounce package frozen chopped spinach, thawed, thoroughly drained, or 1 pound fresh

spinach, washed, drained, and chopped coarsely
6 ounces cream cheese, at room temperature
¼ teaspoon ground nutmeg
Salt and freshly ground black pepper
¼ cup freshly grated Parmesan cheese
1 tablespoon Dijon mustard

Melt the butter in a skillet, add the sausage meat, and cook over medium heat until the meat looses its pinkness, about 5 minutes. Add the onion and sauté for 1 minute longer. Add the mushrooms; continue to cook for another 2 to 3 minutes. Mix in the spinach, making sure it is thoroughly drained, and heat through. If using fresh spinach, add to mushrooms and sauté just until wilted. Remove the pan from the heat. Mash in the softened cream cheese with a fork and add the nutmeg, salt, pepper, Parmesan cheese, and mustard. Mix thoroughly and spread the filling evenly over the warm soufflé.

• Mushroom Leek Soufflé •

¼ pound fresh mushrooms
1 leek
5 tablespoons butter
1 cup milk
3 tablespoons flour
2 tablespoons Dijon
  mustard

4 eggs, separated, plus 1 egg
  white, at room
  temperature
Salt and white pepper to
  taste

Preheat oven to 375 degrees.

Wash and pat the mushrooms dry with paper towels; chop coarsely. Trim the root end of the leek; cut away and discard the tough end of the green part. Thoroughly rinse under cold running water to wash away any soil inside. Slice thinly.

Melt 2 tablespoons of the butter and sauté the mushrooms and leek over medium heat until wilted. Set aside. Bring the milk to a boil in a saucepan and remove from heat.

In a small saucepan melt the remaining 3 tablespoons of butter over low heat and blend in the flour, using a whisk. Stir vigorously for 1 minute until well combined. Remove the pan from the heat and whisk in the milk until smooth. Return the pan to medium heat and continue to cook, stirring, for several minutes, until the sauce is thickened and smooth. Remove the pan from the heat once more, stir in the mustard, and allow to cool slightly.

Beat the egg yolks in a small bowl and add to the cooled sauce. Fold in the mushrooms, leek, salt, and pepper.

Beat the egg whites until they are stiff but not dry. Fold them into the mushroom-leek mixture with a rubber spatula, folding one-half in thoroughly, the second half lightly.

Pour the mixture into a well-buttered four-cup soufflé dish and bake for 35 to 40 minutes, until the soufflé is puffed and browned. Serve immediately.

Serves four.

• Fettuccine with
Mustard Cream Sauce •

¾ pound fresh asparagus
1 cup heavy cream
3 tablespoons Dijon
   mustard
2 tablespoons butter
¼ pound prosciutto ham,*
   thinly sliced, cut into
   ¼-inch-wide strips

1 pound fettuccine (egg
   noodles), preferably fresh*
4 quarts boiling water
1 tablespoon salt
¾ cup freshly grated
   Parmesan cheese
Freshly ground black
   pepper to taste

Break off the tough ends of the asparagus. Rinse stalks well in cold water. In a deep skillet large enough to hold the asparagus lengthwise, bring to a boil about 2 inches of salted water. Add the asparagus and cook, uncovered, for about 6 minutes after the water returns to the boil. The asparagus should be tender but firm. Drain and slice diagonally into ½-inch lengths. Set aside.

Cook the fettuccine while preparing the asparagus. Have ready the boiling water with the tablespoon of salt. Add the fettuccine and cook, stirring with a two-pronged fork, until water returns to the boil. The pasta cooks in 3 to 8 minutes, depending upon whether it is fresh or packaged. Test after 3 minutes. It should be tender but firm. Drain.

In a small bowl beat the heavy cream with the mustard. Wipe dry the same skillet in which the asparagus was cooked. Melt one tablespoon of the butter in the skillet and saute the prosciutto strips over medium-high heat for 1 minute. Add the asparagus pieces, toss with the prosciutto, and add the cooked, drained fettuccine. Toss quickly, adding the remaining tablespoon of butter and the cream-mustard mixture. Turn the heat to high for 30 seconds, until fettuccine is well coated. Remove the pan from the heat and quickly add the Parmesan cheese and a generous amount of freshly ground pepper. Serve immediately with additional Parmesan cheese.

Serves four.

*Available at Italian food specialty stores.

4 tablespoons butter
4 tablespoons olive oil
8 cloves garlic, thinly sliced
1 2-ounce can flat anchovy
  fillets, drained
4 dozen littleneck clams,
  removed from shells or 2
  10-ounce cans whole
  baby clams (reserve clam
  liquor in either case)

2 teaspoons dry mustard
½ cup chopped fresh
  parsley
¼ teaspoon hot red-pepper
  flakes
1 to 1½ pounds linguine
4 to 5 quarts boiling water
1 tablespoon salt

Place the butter and oil in a small saucepan and cook over low heat until the butter melts. Add the sliced garlic and cook for about 5 minutes, until the garlic is soft. Add the anchovy fillets and cook, stirring, until dissolved. Add one cup of the reserved clam liquor, raise the heat to high, and boil for 2 minutes. Lower the heat to simmer and stir in the mustard. Toss in the clams, parsley, and red-pepper flakes. Cook for 3 minutes longer, less if using canned clams. Keep warm over low heat.

To make the linguine, have ready the boiling water with the tablespoon of salt while making the sauce. Add the linguine; stir with a two-pronged fork until the water returns to the boil. Cook, testing after about 3 minutes. The linguine should be tender but firm. Drain and turn out onto a warm serving platter. Pour the clam sauce over it and toss to mix thoroughly. Serve immediately.

Serves four to six.

• For a light snack or Sunday breakfast, toss crumbled sharp cheddar and Dijon mustard to taste (1 teaspoon per egg) into batter for scrambled eggs, serve with warm potato salad (page 184), and garnish with cherry tomatoes and parsley sprigs.

• Vary Eggs Benedict by substituting lightly-sautéed crabmeat for the ham and Mustard Hollandaise (page 169) to coat the poached egg.

• Mix together a cup of olive oil, several chopped fresh tomatoes, lots of oregano or fresh basil leaves, cubed mozzarella, and ¼ cup of Dijon green peppercorn mustard for a cool sauce for hot spaghetti.

• Add a teaspoonful of grainy old-style Dijon mustard to the batter of a two-egg omelet; fill with crumbled bacon, sautéed spinach, and sliced mushrooms.

• Turn a cheese soufflé into a Welsh-Rabbit soufflé by incorporating 2 tablespoons of Dijon mustard and a few dashes of Worcestershire sauce into the cheese mixture before folding in the egg whites.

• Mix a tablespoon or two of Dijon mustard into popover batter, bake as usual, split open, and fill with scrambled eggs spiked with Roquefort cheese.

• Coat the bottom of a partially baked quiche shell with Dijon mustard before adding the filling. Spinach and mushroom quiche is especially good done this way.

• Any creamed sauce destined to top pasta is even more extraordinary with a little Dijon mustard added. Start with a dollop, then go as far as you like.

• Add a tablespoon of Dijon mustard to any savory quiche filling to give it a flavor to savor.

• Vegetable soufflés, such as broccoli and spinach, get an extra lift with the addition of Dijon mustard to taste.

VEGETABLES

• Brussel Sprouts in Mustard Cream •

2 10-ounce packages fresh
  Brussel sprouts
Mustard Cream

Remove all bruised outer leaves from the sprouts and trim the bottoms. Rinse and cook in boiling salted water to cover for 10 to 12 minutes, until tender. Drain, remove to a warm serving dish, and cover with the mustard cream.
Serves four.

MUSTARD CREAM
3 tablespoons butter
3 tablespoons flour
1 cup beef stock
½ cup heavy cream

2 tablespoons Dijon
  mustard
1 teaspoon lemon juice

Melt the butter in a saucepan over medium heat, add the flour, and whisk together for 1 minute until well blended. Add the broth, continuing to stir, then whisk in the cream. Cook over medium heat until the sauce is smooth and thickened, about 5 minutes, whisking constantly. Remove the pan from the heat; stir in the mustard and lemon juice. Pour over the Brussel sprouts and serve immediately.
Makes 1½ cups.

NOTE: Serve over cooked broccoli, cauliflower, and cabbage, or as a sauce for broiled or poached fish.

• Asparagus with Mustard Hollandaise •

1 pound fresh asparagus
Mustard Hollandaise

Wash the asparagus thoroughly, break off the tough ends of the stalks, and pare the bottom two inches with a vegetable parer. In a shallow pan wide enough to hold them flat, place the asparagus in boiling salted water to cover. Cook, uncovered, over medium heat for 8 to 10 minutes, depending upon their thickness. Drain, remove to a serving dish, and cover with Mustard Hollandaise.

Serves four.

MUSTARD HOLLANDAISE

½ cup butter	**2 tablespoons Dijon**
3 egg yolks	**mustard with lemon**
1 tablespoon boiling water	

Melt the butter in a small saucepan and keep it warm. In another small saucepan or the top of a double boiler, combine the egg yolks with the boiling water, whisking over low heat until the yolks begin to thicken. If you are using a double boiler, be sure that the water in the bottom of the boiler never boils. Add the mustard and stir in well. Gradually add the warm melted butter and continue to whisk over low heat for several minutes, until the sauce is thickened and smooth. Pour over the asparagus and serve.

Makes approximately 1 cup.

NOTE: To keep the finished sauce warm you can place the saucepan in a pan of tepid water. If it should curdle, revive it by whisking in a few drops of hot water. Serve over cooked broccoli, cauliflower, Brussel sprouts, or poached eggs.

• Cauliflower in Mustard Bread Crumbs •

2-pound head of
    cauliflower
Mustard Bread Crumbs

Salt and white pepper to
    taste

Rinse the cauliflower well, cutting off the stem and removing the green leaves. Break or cut the head into small flowerets* and soak in cold water for several minutes. Drain.

In a large pot with boiling salted water to cover, cook the cauliflower, covered, simmering for 10 to 15 minutes, until tender. Do not overcook. Drain, place on a warm serving dish, season with salt and pepper. Serve covered with the mustard bread crumbs.

Serves four.

MUSTARD BREAD CRUMBS
4 tablespoons butter
1 clove garlic, crushed
1 tablespoon chopped fresh
    parsley

1½ tablespoons Dijon
    mustard
2 cups fresh bread crumbs

Melt the butter in a small saucepan, add the garlic and parsley, and cook for 1 minute over medium heat, being careful not to burn the garlic. Whisk in the mustard. Add the bread crumbs and toss in the mustard-butter mixture until well coated. Toss with a fork to separate the crumbs. Keep warm in a low (200-degree) oven until ready to use.

Makes 2 cups.

NOTE: Make the bread crumbs from good home-style white bread by putting the slices two at a time into a blender or processor fitted with steel blade. Use several on-off motions, depending upon how coarse or fine you

---

*For a dramatic presentation leave cauliflower whole. Rinse and drain. Cook in boiling salted water to cover, about 20 to 25 minutes.

wish the crumbs. Five slices will yield approximately 2 cups of bread crumbs. They will keep for up to a week in the refrigerator in a well-sealed container. To reheat the mustard bread crumbs, place in a baking pan in a preheated 350-degree oven for 10 minutes. Use on other cooked vegetables such as string beans, broccoli, asparagus, zucchini, Brussel sprouts.

• Glazed Carrots •

1½ pounds carrots
1 tablespoon granulated
  sugar
½ teaspoon salt
2 tablespoons butter
2 tablespoons light-brown
  sugar
¼ teaspoon ground ginger

¼ cup beef stock
2 tablespoons Dijon
  mustard
Salt and white pepper to
  taste
1 tablespoon chopped fresh
  parsley

Scrape and rinse the carrots, cut into 2-inch lengths, then cut each length into julienne strips about ¼-inch wide. Place in a medium saucepan with the granulated sugar and salt, cover with cold water, and bring to a boil over high heat. Lower heat to medium and cook, covered, for about 10 minutes, until carrots are cooked but still firm. Drain.

Melt the butter in a skillet; when sizzling add the carrots and toss over high heat to coat well with the butter. Sprinkle with the brown sugar and ginger, continue cooking, tossing, for several seconds, until carrots begin to glaze.

Whisk together the stock and mustard in a small bowl and pour over the carrots. Lower heat to medium and cook for a few minutes until liquid has cooked down. Season with salt and pepper; sprinkle with parsley before serving.

Serves four.

• Glazed Onions •

4 tablespoons butter
20 small white onions, peeled
½ cup chicken stock
1 tablespoon Dijon mustard with tarragon

Salt and freshly ground black pepper to taste
2 tablespoons light-brown sugar
2 tablespoons chopped fresh parsley

Melt the butter in a skillet large enough to hold the onions in one layer. Sauté the onions for 10 minutes over medium heat, shaking the handle of the pan to coat with butter and brown lightly.

Add the stock and mustard to the pan, cover, and simmer for about 20 minutes, until the onions are soft but firm and most of the liquid has evaporated.

Sprinkle the onions with salt, pepper, and sugar, and cook, uncovered, for an additional 5 minutes, until glazed. Serve sprinkled with parsley.

Serves four.

• Glazed Turnips •

1½ pounds small white turnips
2 tablespoons butter
2 tablespoons light-brown sugar
¼ teaspoon ground ginger
¼ cup beef stock

2 tablespoons Dijon mustard
Salt and white pepper to taste
1 tablespoon chopped fresh parsley

Peel and slice the turnips into ¼-inch thick rounds; cut rounds into quarters.

Melt the butter in a skillet and sauté the turnips over medium heat for about 10 minutes, until tender. Sprinkle the turnips with the sugar and ginger, raise the heat to high, and cook, stirring, for several minutes longer, until they begin to glaze.

Whisk together the stock and mustard in a small bowl and pour over the turnips. Lower heat to medium and cook until the liquid evaporates. Season with salt and pepper and sprinkle with the parsley before serving.

Serves four.

• Braised Celery •

1½ pounds celery hearts
4 tablespoons butter
1 small onion, finely
  chopped
¾ cup beef stock
1 tablespoon chopped fresh
  parsley

1 teaspoon sugar
Salt and freshly ground
  black pepper to taste
1 tablespoon Madeira wine
1 tablespoon Dijon mustard

Trim the root end of the celery, discard the leaves, and cut the stalks into 4-inch lengths.

Melt the butter in a skillet and sauté the onions and celery for 10 minutes over low heat, tossing occasionally.

Add the stock, parsley, sugar, salt, and pepper to the pan. Cover and cook over low heat for 30 minutes. Remove the celery to a warm serving dish with a slotted spoon. Add the Madeira to the liquid in the skillet and boil down over high heat until about ½ cup remains. Remove the pan from the heat, stir in the mustard, and pour the sauce over the celery.

Serves four.

• Try adding a little Dijon mustard to the batter for spinach gnocchi. It's not traditional—but it's pure poetry.

• Spoon dry mustard to taste into a pot of baked beans before serving. Old cookbooks say it makes them less gassy.

• Braised Endive •

8 heads Belgian endive	Salt and freshly ground
4 tablespoons butter	black pepper to taste
¾ cup beef stock	1 tablespoon Madeira wine
1 tablespoon lemon juice	1 tablespoon Dijon mustard
½ teaspoon sugar	

Trim the bottoms of the endive and rinse well; leave endive whole.

Melt the butter in a skillet, add the endive, and sauté for 5 minutes, turning the endive.

Add the stock, lemon juice, sugar, salt, and pepper. Cover and cook over low heat until the endive is tender, about 20 minutes. Remove the endive to a warm serving dish. Add the Madeira to the liquid in the skillet, raise the heat to high, and cook until the liquid is reduced to about ½ cup. Remove the pan from the heat, stir in the mustard, and pour the sauce over the endive.

Serves four.

• Braised Parsnips •

1½ pounds parsnips	1 teaspoon cornstarch
2 tablespoons butter	2 tablespoons Dijon
1 cup beef stock	mustard
½ teaspoon sugar	1 tablespoon chopped fresh
Salt and white pepper to	parsley
taste	

Scrape the parsnips; rinse and cut them in half lengthwise. Cut the lengths into slices about ½-inch thick.

Melt the butter in a skillet, add the parsnips, and toss for about 2 minutes to coat with the butter. Add the stock, sugar, salt, and pepper. Cook, covered, over medium heat for 15 minutes. Remove the parsnips with a slotted spoon to a warm serving dish, leaving the liquid in the skillet. In a small saucer combine the cornstarch with 1 tablespoon of the cooking liquid, then pour this mixture back into the pan. Stir in the mustard and heat for 1 minute, stirring. Pour the sauce over the parsnips, sprinkle with parsley, and serve.

Serves four.

• Scoop out 4 baked potatoes, press through a ricer along with ½ lb. barely cooked fresh (or ½ package defrosted frozen) spinach, mix with ½ pint sour cream or plain yogurt, 2 tablespoons Dijon mustard, and salt and pepper to taste, mound back into skins, and serve with scrambled eggs flecked with slivers of smoked salmon for a late supper or luncheon dish.

• Glaze carrots and turnips with fresh maple syrup and Dijon mustard instead of the usual brown sugar or honey.

• Instead of dull carrots and peas, try sauteéing julienned carrots (3 medium-sized) in butter, and crumbled meat expelled from one link of Italian sweet sausage, sauté for 5 minutes, stirring, until meat browns, add ½ pound julienned green beans; cook, covered, over low heat for about 15 minutes. Just before vegetables are completely tender, stir in a tablespoon of lemon-flavored Dijon mustard, salt, and pepper.

• If you have any sauerkraut left over from Choucroute Garnie (page 134), heat and toss it with cooked buttered egg noodles for a Hungarian-style side dish.

• Cook fresh green beans in boiling salted water till crisp but tender. Drain, toss with butter and freshly cut mustard sprouts, and serve immediately.

• Sweet-and-Sour Red Cabbage •

4 tablespoons butter
1 small onion, finely chopped
1 tablespoon white mustard seeds
2 apples, pared, cored, and diced
3 pounds red cabbage, coarsely shredded

Salt and freshly ground black pepper to taste
1 tablespoon cider vinegar
¼ cup dark-brown sugar, firmly packed
¼ cup spicy brown mustard

In a large skillet melt the butter, add the onion, and sauté over medium heat for 1 minute. Add the mustard seed; continue cooking for a few seconds longer, until the seeds begin to pop. Add the apples and stir to coat with the butter. Cook for 5 minutes. Add the cabbage; season with salt and pepper.

In a small bowl mix together the cider vinegar, brown sugar, and mustard. Pour over the cabbage mixture, raise the heat to high, and boil for 1 minute. Lower heat to medium, cover, and simmer for 15 minutes more. Serve hot.

Serves eight.

• Potatoes Dijon •

2 pounds Idaho potatoes
1 teaspoon salt
Freshly ground black pepper to taste
1 clove garlic, crushed
2 eggs
1 cup heavy cream

⅓ cup Dijon mustard
½ pound imported Swiss or Gruyère cheese, coarsely grated
4 tablespoons butter
¼ cup freshly grated Parmesan cheese

Preheat oven to 375 degrees.

Peel, wash, and slice the potatoes paper-thin. Place them in a large bowl and toss them with the salt, pepper, and garlic.

In a small bowl whisk together the eggs, cream, and mustard until thoroughly combined.

Have ready a well-greased baking dish 10 inches round and 2 inches deep. Place a layer of overlapping potatoes on the bottom, sprinkle with ⅓ of the Swiss cheese, and dot with ⅓ of the butter. Continue to layer in this fashion to make two more layers, ending with the cheese and butter. Pour the cream sauce over the potatoes and sprinkle with the Parmesan cheese.

Cover the baking dish loosely with aluminum foil and bake for 40 minutes. Remove the foil and continue to bake until the potatoes have browned and the custard mixture is firm, about 15 minutes longer.

Serves six.

NOTE: An easy dish to bake ahead and refrigerate. To reheat, bring to room temperature and bake, uncovered, in a preheated 350-degree oven for 30 minutes.

• Spinach Risotto •

1 pound fresh spinach or 1 10-ounce package frozen chopped spinach
½ cup butter (8 tablespoons)
1 clove garlic, finely minced
1 medium onion, finely chopped
5 cups chicken stock
2 cups Italian rice, preferably Arborio brand
½ cup Marsala wine
3 tablespoons Dijon mustard
½ cup freshly grated Parmesan cheese

If you use frozen spinach, do not cook but thaw to room temperature and squeeze out all the liquid. For fresh spinach, pick over the leaves, discard any tough stems, wash, and drain well. Tear into small pieces.

Melt 1 tablespoon of the butter in a skillet, add the garlic, and sauté over medium heat until golden. Add the spinach (frozen or fresh) and sauté together for 1 minute or until fresh spinach is wilted. Set aside.

Melt 5 tablespoons of the butter in a medium saucepan and cook the onion over low heat until it is lightly colored, mixing several times with a wooden spoon. Meanwhile bring the stock to a boil in another saucepan and have it simmering and ready nearby.

Add the rice to the onion-butter mixture and stir until the rice is well coated. Pour in the Marsala and simmer until the liquid is absorbed. Add 1 cup of the stock; continue to stir until it too is absorbed. Continue to add the stock, 1 cup at a time, in the same manner, stirring constantly over low heat. It should take about 20 minutes for the rice to become tender.

Before adding the last cup of stock, fold in the spinach-garlic mixture and mustard and mix thoroughly. Add the final cup of stock. When it is absorbed fold in the remaining 2 tablespoons of butter and the Parmesan cheese. Texture should be creamy.

Serve at once, with additional freshly grated cheese. Serves six.

NOTE: Do not attempt this dish with anything but Italian rice and imported Parmesan cheese. The results just aren't the same.

• Yam Casserole •

---

6 medium-sized yams, about 2 pounds	½ cup heavy cream
4 tablespoons butter	1 teaspoon salt
6 tablespoons dark-brown sugar	¼ cup dark rum
	Grated rind of 1 orange
	½ cup Dusseldorf mustard

Preheat oven to 350 degrees.

Wash the yams well, leaving skins on. Place them in a large heavy pot with cold salted water to cover. Bring to a boil over high heat, cover, and cook over medium heat until tender when pierced with a fork. Cooking time will vary between 15 to 25 minutes, depending upon size of the yams. Drain and peel when cool enough to handle.

In a blender or a processor fitted with steel blade, puree the yams, adding 2 tablespoons of the butter, 4 tablespoons of the brown sugar, the cream, salt, rum, orange rind, and mustard. Blend for 1 minute or until smooth.

Place in a well-buttered 2-quart casserole and dot with a mixture of the remaining 2 tablespoons each of the butter and brown sugar. Bake for 30 minutes.

Serves six to eight.

• Stir-fry vegetables in a little mustard oil with garlic and a touch of ginger. Season with light soy sauce.

• Steam new potatoes in their pink jackets and dress with Mustard Butter (page 193) and snipped fresh dill.

• A little grated Parmesan or sharp cheddar incorporated with a teaspoon or two of Dijon mustard into plain mashed potatoes can lift them out of the ordinary.

• As an appetizer or to accompany a roast or grilled meat, try stuffing onions or zucchini with a mixture of Italian sweet sausage meat, mushrooms, and bread crumbs, all sautéed, then bound with heavy cream, Parmesan cheese, and a tablespoon or two of Dijon mustard. Stuff the vegetables and bake in a 350-degree oven, adding a cup of chicken stock to the pan.

• Don't throw away those artichoke stems! Cut them from Italian globe artichokes, peel, slice thin, and sauté in oil and garlic; remove from heat and, add a tablespoon of lemon-flavored Dijon.

SALADS

• Beet Salad •

12 to 14 whole fresh
    medium-sized beets
¼ cup cider vinegar
2 teaspoons sugar
¼ cup Dijon mustard
2 tablespoons white
    mustard seeds

3 tablespoons chopped
    fresh parsley
Salt and freshly ground
    black pepper to taste
3 scallions, thinly sliced,
    green included

Wash and trim the beets, leaving one inch of stem and the root ends. Place the beets in cold salted water to cover halfway and bring to a boil over high heat. Lower the heat to medium and cook, covered, for about 45 minutes, or until the beets are fork-tender. Drain in a colander and cool.

When the beets are cool enough to handle, slip off the skins; trim and slice beets crosswise into thin rounds. Place in a serving bowl.

In a small bowl combine the cider vinegar, sugar, and mustard, and whisk until the dressing is creamy. Mix in the mustard seeds, parsley, salt, and pepper, and pour the dressing over the beets. Toss to coat the beets well. Sprinkle with the chopped scallions and allow to marinate for several hours in the refrigerator before serving.

Serves six.

• Cucumber Salad •

4 medium cucumbers
1 tablespoon coarse
  (kosher) salt
1 cup plain yogurt
2 tablespoons Dijon
  mustard
2 tablespoons olive oil
½ teaspoon salt

Freshly ground black
  pepper to taste
1 tablespoon red wine
  vinegar
1 clove garlic, crushed
3 tablespoons snipped fresh
  dill

Pare the cucumbers or wash the skins thoroughly if you prefer to leave them on. Slice them as thin as possible. Place the slices in a colander, sprinkle and toss with the coarse salt, and allow them to drain for 1 hour. Dry the slices on paper towels.

Place the yogurt in a small bowl; whisk in the mustard, oil, salt, pepper, vinegar, garlic, and dill. Fold in the cucumbers gently and mix until thoroughly coated with the dressing. Transfer to a serving bowl and chill before serving.

Serves six.

• Lentil Salad •

1 pound dried lentils
6 cups cold water
1 medium onion stuck with
  2 cloves
1 bay leaf, split in half
1 teaspoon salt
1 medium red onion, finely
  chopped
¼ cup chopped fresh
  parsley

½ cup coarsely chopped
  pimiento, drained
3 tablespoons Dijon
  mustard
1 large clove garlic, crushed
¼ cup tarragon vinegar
¾ cup olive oil
Salt and freshly ground
  black pepper to taste

Place the lentils, water, whole onion stuck with cloves, bay leaf, and salt in a large pot. Simmer, covered, over medium heat for 40 minutes. Have a colander ready in the sink and drain the lentils. Discard the onion and bay leaf and rinse the lentils briefly under cold running water. Drain and transfer to a large serving bowl. Add the chopped onion, parsley, and pimiento.

In a small bowl mix together the mustard, garlic, and vinegar. Add the oil gradually, mixing as you add. Pour the dressing over the lentil salad, add the salt and pepper, and toss to coat thoroughly with the dressing. Allow to marinate for an hour or two before serving at room temperature.

Serves twelve or more.

• Creamy Coleslaw •

2 to 2½ pounds cabbage, finely shredded
1 large onion, finely chopped
3 tablespoons chopped fresh parsley
1¼ cups mayonnaise
½ cup Dijon mustard
1 large clove garlic, crushed
1 teaspoon salt
1 tablespoon sugar
2 tablespoons red wine vinegar
1 teaspoon celery seeds
1 tablespoon white mustard seeds
1 teaspoon Worcestershire sauce
Freshly ground black pepper to taste
Optional: 1 green bell pepper, seeded and finely chopped

Place the cabbage (and green pepper, if desired), onion and parsley in a large mixing bowl.

In a small bowl combine all the remaining ingredients and whisk together.

Pour the dressing over the vegetables and mix with a rubber spatula to coat the salad thoroughly. Taste for seasoning, add additional salt, if necessary, and a generous amount of freshly ground pepper. Refrigerate for several hours before serving.

Serves six to eight.

• Sweet-and-Sour Coleslaw •

2 pounds cabbage, finely
   shredded
1 large onion, finely
   chopped
½ cup sugar
1 teaspoon salt
½ cup cider vinegar
¼ cup vegetable oil

2 teaspoons dry mustard
1 tablespoon white mustard
   seeds
2 eggs
2 tablespoons chopped
   fresh parsley
Freshly ground black
   pepper to taste

Place the cabbage and onion in a large mixing bowl.

In a small saucepan mix together the sugar, salt, vinegar, oil, mustard, and mustard seed, and bring to a boil, stirring, until the sugar dissolves. Remove pan from the heat.

In a small bowl beat the eggs and stir in 2 tablespoons of the boiled dressing. Gradually add the beaten eggs to the saucepan and return the dressing to medium heat, whisking for several minutes, until it begins to thicken. Do not let it boil. Remove from heat immediately and pour over the cabbage-and-onion mixture. Add the parsley and toss well to coat the vegetables thoroughly.

Allow the salad to stand until it reaches room temperature. Taste for seasoning. Add more salt, if necessary, and freshly ground pepper. Chill before serving.

Serves six to eight.

NOTE: Making this salad 24 hours before serving gives the mustard flavor even more time to develop.

2 pounds small new
  red-skinned potatoes
1 small onion, coarsely
  chopped

½ pound fresh string beans
¼ pound sliced bacon
Freshly ground black
  pepper

Wash the potatoes well, do not peel, and place in a saucepan with cold salted water to cover. Bring to a boil and cook over medium heat until tender, 15 to 20 minutes. Drain, quarter, leaving skins on, and place in a large serving bowl along with the onion.

Rinse and trim the string beans; cut diagonally into 1-inch lengths. Place in boiling salted water to cover and cook, uncovered, for 10 minutes, until barely tender. Drain and add to the potatoes and onion.

Fry the bacon until crisp but not burned. Drain on paper towels and crumble into small pieces. Set aside.

Pour the dressing over the salad and mix with a rubber spatula, taking care not to crumble the potatoes. Top with the bacon and lots of freshly ground black pepper.

Serve while still warm.

Serves six.

DRESSING

½ cup beef stock
2 tablespoons wine vinegar
2 teaspoons dry mustard
1 tablespoon Dijon mustard
1 teaspoon salt

Generous splash of bottled
  Maggi seasoning*
3 tablespoons chopped
  fresh parsley
6 tablespoons olive oil

Place the beef stock, wine vinegar, dry mustard, prepared mustard, salt, Maggi, and parsley in a bowl. Whisk together until combined; gradually whisk in the oil.

Makes approximately ¾ cup.

*Available at most supermarkets.

• Tomato and Mustard-Sprout Salad •

4 large ripe tomatoes
½ pound fresh mozzarella
  cheese, thinly sliced
½ cup mustard sprouts

Slice each tomato into eight wedges. Place in a serving bowl along with the sliced cheese and mustard sprouts. Toss with Mustard Vinaigrette Dressing (page 188).
Serves four.

NOTE: Mustard sprouts are not available at greengrocers but are easily grown on any sunny windowsill. (See page 78) They have a fresh, pungent, mustardy taste. The seeds sprout in two days and are ready to harvest in four.

• Secret Ingredient Potato Salad •

3 pounds boiling potatoes
1 large Bermuda onion,
  finely chopped
2 teaspoons salt
Freshly ground black
  pepper to taste

3 tablespoons chopped
  fresh parsley
2 tablespoons dry mustard
½ cup cold water
1¼ cups mayonnaise

Wash the potatoes thoroughly and place them in a large saucepan with cold water to cover. Bring the liquid to a boil over high heat, lower the heat, and simmer, covered, for 25 minutes or until the potatoes are tender but firm. Drain and cool.

When the potatoes are cool enough to handle, peel and slice them crosswise into ⅛-inch rounds. Place in a large bowl with the onion, salt, pepper, and parsley.

In a small bowl whisk the dry mustard with the water until dissolved. Gradually whisk in the mayonnaise until the dressing is smooth. Pour the dressing over the potatoes and mix gently and thoroughly with a wooden spoon to coat all surfaces of the potatoes. Break up some of the potatoes as you mix for a creamier texture. Chill for several hours before serving.

Serves eight.

NOTE: Although the potato salad may be served as soon as it is chilled, it is best when made 24 hours ahead, allowing all the flavors to meld. Water, not mustard, is the secret ingredient here, giving the potatoes a creamy, moist consistency.

• One of the most refreshing summer dishes is chopped radishes, cucumbers, scallions, and green peppers with lots of freshly ground pepper, salt, and plenty of sour cream. Serve sprinkled with mustard sprouts and it's even better.

• If you like spinach-and-mushroom salad, use the recipe for Marinated Mushrooms (page 93) to dress the leaves; add crumbled bacon if you like.

• Add bright mustardy flavor to salads and sautéed or steamed vegetables by tossing in a handful of the tiny pale-green leaves and delicate white stems of *home-sprouted* white mustard seeds.

• Substitute chick peas for lentils in the recipe for Lentil Salad (page 181); add a handful of mustard sprouts and tiny cubes of mozzarella cheese. Decorate with tiny cooked shrimp.

SAUCES, DRESSINGS, AND CONDIMENTS

• Basic Salad Dressing •

2 teaspoons dry mustard	Generous dash of bottled
2 tablespoons red wine	Maggi seasoning*
vinegar	Salt and freshly ground
6 tablespoons olive oil	black pepper to taste

In a small bowl whisk together the mustard and vinegar until the mustard is dissolved. Gradually whisk in the oil until well combined. Whisk in the Maggi, salt, and pepper. Store in the refrigerator in a well-sealed jar. Shake well before using. The dressing will keep indefinitely in the refrigerator.

Mustard strength may be increased according to personal taste. Vary the dressing with the addition of any fresh or dried herbs and/or crushed fresh garlic. An herb vinegar or flavored oil can be substituted, but keep the ratio of 3 parts oil to 1 part vinegar.

Makes approximately ½ cup, or enough for four servings.

NOTE: To make the dressing in larger amounts, place all the ingredients in the container of a blender or processor fitted with steel blade. Process for 1 minute.

*Available at most supermarkets.

• Mustard Salad Dressing •

1 egg
¼ cup red wine vinegar
1 teaspoon salt
Freshly ground black
  pepper to taste
1 large clove garlic, crushed

2 tablespoons Dijon
  mustard
1 tablespoon chopped fresh
  parsley
¾ cup olive oil

Place the egg in a small bowl and whisk briefly. Add the vinegar, salt, pepper, garlic, mustard, and parsley, and whisk until combined. Add the oil gradually in a stream, whisking until dressing is creamy.

To make in a blender or processor fitted with steel blade, place all ingredients in the container. Leave garlic and parsley sprigs whole. Run the motor for 1 minute to blend all ingredients. The dressing will keep for 1 week in a well-sealed container in the refrigerator.

Makes approximately 1⅓ cups.

• Mustard Vinaigrette •

2 tablespoons Dijon
  mustard
2 tablespoons red wine
  vinegar
Salt and freshly ground
  black pepper to taste

1 medium clove garlic,
  crushed
½ cup olive oil

Place the mustard in a small bowl with the vinegar, salt, pepper, and garlic, and whisk until creamy. Gradually add the oil, whisking until it is completely absorbed.

To make in a blender or processor fitted with steel blade, place all ingredients in the container, leaving garlic clove whole. Process for 30 seconds.

To vary the taste of the dressing, add any favorite herbs, fresh or dried, such as tarragon, basil, rosemary, parsley, or a combination—or substitute any herb mustard for the plain mustard. The dressing can be refrigerated for several weeks in a well-sealed container.

This can also be used as a dressing for cold cooked or raw vegetables, cold meat, or fish.

Makes approximately ½ cup.

• Tartar Sauce •

1 egg yolk
2 tablespoons Dijon
  mustard
1 tablespoon red wine
  vinegar
1 cup olive oil
1 teaspoon Worcestershire
  sauce
1 tablespoon chopped fresh
  parsley

2 tablespoons shallots,
  finely chopped
2 tablespoons sweet
  gherkins, finely chopped
1 tablespoon capers,
  drained, finely chopped
Dash of Tabasco

Place the egg yolk, mustard, and vinegar in a small bowl. With a whisk gradually beat in the oil, drop by drop, as in making mayonnaise. When all the oil has been used and the sauce is thickened, fold in the Worcestershire, parsley, shallots, gherkins, capers, and Tabasco.

To make in a blender or a processor fitted with steel blade the method is the same. Place the first 3 ingredients in the container. With motor running slowly add the oil and blend for 1 minute until creamy. Add other ingredients and use a quick on-off motion to blend them into the sauce. It will keep in a well-sealed container, refrigerated, for two weeks.

Serve with hot or cold seafood, broiled or poached fish, deep-fried shellfish or fish, or use as a sandwich spread.

Makes 1¼ cups.

• Herb Sauce •

3 tablespoons Dijon
  mustard
1 teaspoon anchovy paste
1 clove garlic, crushed
⅓ cup red wine vinegar
1 cup olive oil
1 small boiled potato,
  peeled, chilled
1 small onion, finely
  chopped

1 tablespoon capers,
  drained, finely chopped
1 tablespoon sweet
  gherkins, finely chopped
1 teaspoon dried or
  1 tablespoon fresh tarragon
2 tablespoons chopped
  pimiento
1 hard-cooked egg, coarsely
  chopped

In a bowl combine the mustard, anchovy paste, garlic, and vinegar, and whisk together thoroughly. Gradually whisk in the oil until the sauce is creamy. Crumble the potato and mix it in. Fold in the onion, capers, gherkins, tarragon, and pimiento with a rubber spatula. Last, fold in the egg. The sauce will keep for several days in a well-sealed container in the refrigerator. Bring to room temperature and stir before serving.

Serve with cold or hot boiled meats, fish, and vegetables.
Makes approximately 1½ cups.

• Pickled Mustard Sauce •

½ cup Dijon mustard
½ cup spicy brown mustard
⅓ cup kosher-style pickles,
  finely chopped

⅓ cup sweet gherkins,
  finely chopped
1 teaspoon Worcestershire
  sauce

Combine the two mustards in a small bowl, add the chopped pickles and gherkins, and mix well. Add the Worcestershire sauce. This will keep indefinitely in a well-sealed container in the refrigerator.

Serve with cold cuts, boiled meats, and as a sandwich spread.

Makes about 1 cup.

• Watercress Sauce •

1 large bunch watercress
16 ounces sour cream or
  plain yogurt

½ cup Dijon mustard
2 teaspoons bottled white
  horseradish, drained

Wash the watercress and dry it thoroughly on paper towels. Remove and discard any fat, tough stems. Place the watercress in the container of a blender or processor fitted with steel blade. Using a few quick on-off motions, coarsely chop the watercress. Add the sour cream, mustard, and horseradish, and process for 30 seconds.

Serve as a dip for cold vegetables, raw or cooked; as a sauce for cold salmon, any cold fish, or cold chicken.

Makes 1½ cups.

• Mustard Dill Sauce •

½ cup Dijon mustard
½ cup spicy brown mustard
⅓ cup sugar

⅓ cup vegetable oil
1 large bunch fresh dill,
  finely snipped

In a small bowl, using a wire whisk, combine the two mustards. Add the sugar gradually, whisking until it is dissolved. Gradually add the oil, whisking until it is completely absorbed. Fold in the dill.

Serve with gravlax or as a dressing for cold shrimp or lobster.

Makes 1½ cups.

• Blender Mayonnaise •

2 egg yolks	1 tablespoon lemon juice
1 teaspoon salt	1½ cups vegetable or olive
1 teaspoon Dijon mustard	oil, or a mixture of both

In a blender on high speed, or in a processor fitted with steel blade, process the egg yolks for 30 seconds, until they thicken slightly. Add the salt, mustard, and lemon juice and process for 30 seconds longer. With the motor running add the oil, drop by drop, until about one-half cup has been incorporated and the mayonnaise has started to thicken. It is safe at this point to start adding the balance of the oil in a slow, steady stream until it is all absorbed and the mayonnaise is smooth and creamy.

Makes approximately 1½ to 2 cups.

NOTE: It is most important when making mayonnaise that all ingredients be at room temperature. If the mayonnaise separates or refuses to thicken it may be remedied in the following manner:

Pour the mixture into a bowl. Rinse the container of blender or processor with warm water and dry it thoroughly. Place one teaspoon of Dijon mustard and one teaspoon of the separated mayonnaise in the container. Process for 30 seconds. Then begin adding, drop by drop, the separated mayonnaise. When it begins to thicken once again, add the balance in a steady stream. The mayonnaise will keep, refrigerated, for up to 2 weeks in a well-sealed container.

• Mustard Mayonnaise •

To the blender mayonnaise add one or more tablespoons of imported Dijon mustard, depending upon your taste. Add the additional mustard after the mayonnaise is completely thickened.

• Mustard Butter •

½ cup butter, at room
   temperature
2 tablespoons prepared
   mustard

1 teaspoon lemon juice
Optional: Chopped fresh
   parsley

Place the butter in a small bowl and cream with a
wooden spoon. Gradually beat in the mustard until it is
completely absorbed. Add the lemon juice and parsley.

To make in larger quantities, use a blender or processor
fitted with steel blade. Place all the ingredients in the
container and process for 30 seconds. Scrape down the sides
with a rubber spatula and process again.

Keep this mixture in a well-sealed container in the
refrigerator, where it will keep for several weeks. It may also
be frozen. It is wonderful to have on hand for the following:
spread on cold-cut sandwiches and smoked salmon canapes.
Spread on steak, fish, or chicken before broiling. Use for
scrambling eggs; on toast for poached eggs. Add garlic and
use for garlic bread. Melt over boiled vegetables. Vary the
taste by using a variety of mustard flavors—either
homemade or bottled. Add herbs to taste or try herb
mustards.

Makes ½ cup.

• Mustard Soy Dipping Sauce •

2 tablespoons dry mustard
2 tablespoons white vinegar
   or rice wine vinegar

1 clove garlic, crushed
½ cup soy sauce

Place the dry mustard in a small bowl. Gradually whisk in
the vinegar to form a paste. Add the garlic, and then the
soy sauce in a slow stream, whisking constantly until the
mixture is completely smooth and all the ingredients are
well blended. The sauce will be thin. Allow it to stand at

room temperature for at least 10 minutes before using, for the flavor to develop.

Serve with batter-fried shrimp, any batter-fried vegetable, spareribs.

Makes ½ cup.

NOTE: To make in greater quantities, place all ingredients in the container of a blender or processor fitted with steel blade. Leave the garlic whole. Process for 1 minute, until all ingredients are combined.

• Deviled Sauce I •

2 tablespoons butter
1 medium onion, finely chopped
1 large clove garlic, finely minced
2 tablespoons red wine vinegar
⅓ cup dry red wine
3 teaspoons cornstarch
2 cups beef stock
⅛ teaspoon cayenne pepper

Salt and freshly ground black pepper to taste
1 tablespoon tomato paste
¼ teaspoon anchovy paste
1 tablespoon light corn syrup
4 tablespoons Dijon mustard
Optional: ¼ cup heavy cream

Melt the butter in a small saucepan. Add the onion and garlic and cook slowly over low heat until transparent. Add the vinegar, raise the heat to high, and boil rapidly until the vinegar is almost evaporated. Add the wine and continue to cook over high heat for 2 to 3 minutes longer.

In a small bowl blend the cornstarch with one tablespoon of the stock and whisk until cornstarch is dissolved. Add the remainder of the stock and mix thoroughly. Pour into the onion mixture, add the cayenne pepper, salt, and pepper, and cook over low heat for 10 minutes, until sauce thickens. Stir occasionally. Add the tomato paste, anchovy paste, and corn syrup; mix and simmer for 5 minutes longer. Remove the pan from the heat and stir in the mustard. Add cream, if desired, at this point, and heat briefly; do not boil.

Serve with Deviled Spareribs, Deviled Beef Bones, broiled fish, or as a barbecue sauce.

Makes approximately 2 cups.

• Deviled Sauce II •

1 6-ounce bottle Sauce
  Diable (Escoffier label)*
¼ cup beef stock

¼ cup Dijon mustard
Optional: ¼ to ½ cup
  heavy cream

Put Sauce Diable into a small saucepan. Pour the beef stock into the bottle, cap it, and shake thoroughly to get all the remaining contents from the bottle. Add this to the saucepan. Whisk in the mustard and place over low heat for 5 minutes, stirring, until heated through. At this point add the heavy cream, if desired. Heat briefly; do not boil. Add cream according to taste, but try the sauce both ways.

Use as a sauce with any broiled, deviled meat or chicken, deep-fried chicken or fish, or as a barbecue sauce.

Makes approximately 1 cup.

*Available at most supermarkets.

• Here is a diet salad-dressing equally as satisfying as any calorie-stuffed oil-based recipe: lemon juice, powdered or Dijon mustard, Worcestershire sauce, Maggi seasoning, and salt and pepper, all to taste. Skip the salt and use a salt-free mustard for low-sodium diets.

• Add prepared mustard to bottled chutney and vegetable relishes to heighten the taste.

• Barbecue Sauce •

2 tablespoons vegetable oil
1 large onion, coarsely
  chopped
2 cloves garlic, finely
  minced
1 cup canned tomato sauce
¼ cup cider vinegar

¼ cup light corn syrup
½ cup Dijon mustard with
  lemon
3 tablespoons
  Worcestershire sauce
½ teaspoon Tabasco

Heat the oil in a saucepan. Add the onion and garlic and sauté over low heat for 5 minutes. Add the tomato sauce, vinegar, corn syrup, mustard, Worcestershire sauce, and Tabasco, mix thoroughly, and continue to cook over low heat for 10 minutes.

Spread on spareribs, chicken, and meats, when barbecuing.

Makes 2½ cups.

• Basic Mustard Bechamel Sauce •

2 tablespoons butter
3 tablespoons flour
1 cup milk
Salt and freshly ground
  black pepper to taste

2 tablespoons prepared
  mustard

Melt the butter in a small saucepan over medium heat. Whisk in the flour until well blended. In a separate pan scald the milk, then add it gradually to the butter-flour mixture and continue to whisk until smooth and thickened. Add salt and pepper. Remove the pan from the heat and whisk in the mustard. Use flavored mustards, depending upon recipe. Try tarragon mustard with chicken, lemon mustard for vegetables, basil mustard for pasta.

Serve on blanched vegetables, poached eggs, crepes; add

Parmesan cheese and serve on pasta; use as a base for soufflés and for other sauces such as Mornay.

Makes 1 cup.

• Mustard Velouté Sauce •

Use the same proportions and method as for bechamel sauce, but substitute chicken, beef, or fish stock for the milk. This depends on recipe being used. Proceed as above, remove pan from the heat, and whisk in the mustard.

Serve on poached fish and chicken, or as a base for soups and other sauces.

Makes 1 cup.

• Creamy Mustard Sauce •

3 eggs
1 cup heavy cream
¼ cup vegetable oil
1 tablespoon red wine
  vinegar

6 tablespoons Dijon
  mustard

Place all the ingredients in a small heavy pot, whisk together until well combined, and cook over low heat until thickened, about 5 minutes. Do not allow the mixture to boil. If you are not using the sauce hot, cool, place in a well-sealed container, and refrigerate. It will keep for about 1 week.

Serve hot with broiled fish or chicken, steamed vegetables. Serve cold with cold seafood, raw vegetables, cold meats and chicken. Add your favorite herbs to vary the taste. Try fresh dill with fish, rosemary with chicken, tarragon with vegetables.

Makes 2 cups.

• Rosemary Mustard Sauce •

2 tablespoons butter
3 tablespoons flour
6 tablespoons Dijon
  mustard
1½ cups chicken stock
½ cup dry sherry

1 teaspoon Worcestershire
  sauce
¼ cup fresh rosemary
  leaves, or 1 teaspoon
  dried

Melt the butter in a small saucepan. Add the flour and whisk together over medium heat for 1 minute. Add the mustard and whisk in until combined. Gradually add the stock, continue to cook, and whisk continuously until the sauce is smooth and thickened, about 5 minutes. Stir in the sherry, Worcestershire sauce, and rosemary leaves, and simmer over low heat 5 minutes longer.

Serve with roast fresh ham, roast leg of lamb, roast beef, broiled fish.

Makes approximately 1½ cups.

• Mustard Mint Sauce •

3 egg yolks
4 tablespoons Dijon
  mustard with lemon
1 teaspoon cornstarch
½ teaspoon salt

1 cup chicken stock
1 small bunch fresh mint,
  finely chopped (about 4
  tablespoons)*

Combine the egg yolks, mustard, cornstarch, and salt in a small heavy pot or the top of a double boiler. Whisk together thoroughly.

Stirring constantly, gradually add the stock and cook over medium heat for about 10 minutes, or until just thickened. Do not allow the mixture to boil. Keep the

*One tablespoon dried mint may be substituted, but do not expect the same fresh, minty result.

sauce warm until it is ready to use. Stir in the fresh mint before serving.

Serve with roast or grilled lamb or fish.

Makes about 1 cup.

Some multipurpose sauce recipes appear in conjunction with other recipes in this book.

REMOULADE SAUCE, see page 85
This is good with cold cooked shellfish, fried seafood, and raw vegetables.

MUSTARD VINEGAR SAUCE, see page 123
Nice with cold meats or cold seafood.

EGG MUSTARD SAUCE, see page 151
This can be served with any baked or poached fish; also good on hot, boiled shrimp, poached chicken, or cooked vegetables.

MUSTARD CREAM, see page 168
Use over cooked broccoli, cauliflower, and cabbage, or as a sauce for broiled or poached fish.

MUSTARD HOLLANDAISE, see page 169
Excellent addition to cooked broccoli, cauliflower, Brussel sprouts, or poached eggs.

MUSTARD BREAD CRUMBS, see page 170
Serve with cooked vegetables such as string beans, broccoli, asparagus, zucchini, Brussel sprouts.

3 large ripe mangoes, peeled, pitted, diced in small pieces (approximately 8 cups)
1 small green bell pepper, diced in small pieces
1 small red bell pepper, diced in small pieces
1 medium onion, coarsely chopped
1 cup toasted pecans, coarsely chopped
3 tablespoons fresh ginger root, peeled and finely grated
Rind of 2 oranges, finely chopped
1 cup cider vinegar
1 tablespoon white mustard seeds
1 teaspoon salt
2 cups sugar
2 cups golden seedless raisins
½ cup prepared hot English mustard (page 74)*

In a large pot combine all the ingredients except the mustard. Place over high heat and bring to a rolling boil, stirring constantly with a wooden spoon. Reduce the heat to low and simmer for 30 minutes, stirring frequently.

Spoon about 1 cup of the chutney into a small bowl and add the mustard to it, mixing until thoroughly incorporated. Pour this mixture back into the pot of chutney and mix well. Ladle the hot mixture into hot, sterilized jars, seal, and store in a cool place.

Makes ten ½-pint jars.

NOTE: To sterilize jars, wash the jars and lids well in hot, sudsy water, rinse with hot water, and put them in a large pot with hot water to cover. Bring the water to a boil, boil for 5 minutes, and turn off the heat, allowing the jars and lids to stand in the hot water. Just before filling, invert the jars onto a clean dry towel. Fill and seal the jars one at a time, while they are still hot. Do not fill more than ⅛-inch from the top. Allow the jars to cool before storing. When using the "Mason" jar type with lid and ring top, a properly sealed lid will have a slight indentation in the center that will not pop back when pressed. Any jar not properly sealed

*Or use prepared bottled hot English mustard.

may be stored in the refrigerator for more immediate use. In pickling and preserving, the safest procedure is to carefully follow the manufacturer's instructions.

• Cranberry Relish •

2 pounds fresh whole
  cranberries
2 whole oranges
1 cup water
1 cup sugar

2 tablespoons crystallized
  ginger
3 tablespoons spicy brown
  mustard

Rinse the cranberries in a colander and drain well.

Cut the oranges into quarters and remove any seeds. In a blender or a processor fitted with steel blade coarsely chop the oranges, rind included, using several quick on-off motions.

Place the cranberries, oranges, water, and sugar in a large saucepan and bring to a boil over high heat, cooking for several minutes, until cranberries pop. Lower the heat to medium and cook, covered, for 15 minutes longer, stirring occasionally. Remove the pan from the heat and cool slightly.

Mix in thoroughly the crystallized ginger and the mustard. Store in a glass or plastic container with tight-fitting lid. The relish will keep for several weeks in the refrigerator. It may also be stored in the freezer.

Makes 6 cups.

• Mustard Pear Relish •

3 pounds ripe Bartlett pears	½ tablespoon fresh ginger
1 cup sugar	root, peeled, finely grated
Grated rind of 1 lemon	½ cup golden raisins
Juice of 1 lemon	3 tablespoons dry mustard

Peel and core the pears. Dice finely.

Place them in a large saucepan along with the remaining ingredients. Bring to a boil over high heat, lower the heat, and simmer for 20 minutes, stirring occasionally. Ladle the hot mixture into sterilized jars, following the directions on page 200. The relish will keep in a well-sealed container, refrigerated, for up to a month.

Serve as you would a chutney.

Makes approximately 1 quart.

• Marinated Mustard Peppers •

6 large green bell peppers	1 teaspoon salt
½ cup white vinegar	1 teaspoon sugar
1 tablespoon pickling spices	4 teaspoons dry mustard

Halve the peppers; core, seed, and rinse them well. Cut into strips about ½-inch wide.

Put the peppers in a heavy skillet large enough to hold them in one layer. Do not add water; the water clinging to them is enough for cooking them. Steam, covered, for about 10 minutes over low heat. Remove pan from heat and allow to stand, covered.

In a small bowl whisk together the vinegar, pickling spices, salt, sugar, and mustard until well blended. Pour this mixture over the peppers, replace cover, and allow to stand for about 1 hour, until they reach room temperature. Store in glass or plastic container with tight-fitting lid and keep refrigerated. Marinate for 24 hours before serving.

Serve as a side dish with cold meats.

Makes 5 to 6 cups.

• Mustard Vegetable Relish •

1½-pound head of
  cauliflower
1 pound string beans
2 tablespoons salt
¾ cup sugar
2 tablespoons white
  mustard seeds
½ cup dry mustard
1 tablespoon ground
  turmeric
¼ teaspoon cayenne pepper

¾ cup flour
4 cups cider vinegar
2 large cucumbers,
  unpeeled, diced in small
  pieces
3 medium green bell
  peppers, diced in small
  pieces
3 medium onions, coarsely
  chopped

Rinse the cauliflower well, cut off the stem, and remove the green leaves. Break into small flowerets. Cook for 5 minutes in boiling salted water to cover, and drain. Set aside.

Rinse and trim the string beans. Cut them into 2-inch lengths. Cook in boiling salted water to cover, until just barely tender, about 10 minutes. Drain and set aside.

Place the salt, sugar, mustard seeds, dry mustard, turmeric, cayenne pepper, flour, and cider vinegar in a large pot, and whisk together until smooth. Cook over medium heat, stirring constantly, until thickened, about 5 minutes.

Add the cauliflower, string beans, cucumbers, peppers, and onions to the sauce, and mix to combine thoroughly. Bring the mixture to a boil over high heat, lower heat, and simmer for 15 minutes.

Pack into hot, sterilized jars, following the directions on page 200, or store in well-sealed containers, refrigerated, for more immediate use.

Serve as an accompaniment to hot or cold meat dishes. Makes 3 quarts.

• Mustard Peanut Butter •

2 cups salted peanuts
2 tablespoons Dijon
   mustard

Generous pinch of cayenne
   pepper
1 tablespoon peanut oil

Place all the ingredients in container of a blender or processor fitted with steel blade. Use quick on-off motions until the nuts are ground fine, then let the motor run until a paste is formed, stopping to scrape down the sides of the bowl several times with a spatula. Pack into a well-sealed jar and keep refrigerated. Keeps indefinitely.

Use as a spread for sandwiches or crackers.

Makes approximately 1¼ cups.

• For a quick barbecue sauce combine soy sauce, minced garlic, and lemon juice with Tomato Herb Mustard (page 76).

• Creamed sauces for broiled food are given immediate and welcome zip by the addition of Dijon, mustard (a teaspoonful or more to taste).

• For a quick and easy sauce for seafood and poached chicken breasts or croquettes, puree cooked peas, broccoli, cauliflower, zucchini, or other vegetables in a food processor or blender. Add salt, pepper, and a tablespoon of lemon-flavored Dijon mustard; process 30 seconds longer.

BAKING

• Nut Cookies •

2½ cups all-purpose flour
1 teaspoon baking soda
½ teaspoon salt
1 cup butter, at room
   temperature
½ teaspoon cinnamon
½ teaspoon allspice
2 teaspoons dry mustard

1 teaspoon vanilla
1½ cups granulated sugar
3 eggs, at room temperature
1 cup currants
1½ cups pecans, coarsely
   chopped
1½ cups confectioners
   sugar

Preheat oven to 375 degrees.

Sift together the flour, baking soda, and salt. Set aside.

In the large bowl of an electric mixer cream the butter. Beat in the cinnamon, allspice, mustard, and vanilla. Gradually add the granulated sugar and beat well. Add the eggs, one at a time, beating well after each addition. Scrape the sides of the bowl frequently with a rubber spatula. Turn the mixer to the lowest speed and add the sifted flour mixture. Beat briefly, just to blend the flour with the other ingredients. Stir in the currants and pecans on low speed, or by hand with a rubber spatula.

Place by heaping teaspoonsful about 2 inches apart on unbuttered cookie sheets. Bake for 10 to 12 minutes until well browned. Halfway during the baking time, turn the cookie sheets around to insure even baking. Remove the cookies to a cooling rack immediately. While still warm, roll them in the confectioners sugar. After cookies have cooled, transfer to a tin for storage.

Makes approximately 7 dozen cookies.

• Mustard Molasses Cookies •

2½ cups all-purpose flour
¾ teaspoon baking soda
6 tablespoons butter, at
  room temperature
½ cup granulated sugar
½ cup light-brown sugar,
  firmly packed

⅓ cup unsulfured molasses
1 teaspoon dry mustard
1 teaspoon white vinegar
1 egg, at room temperature

Sift together the flour and baking soda and set aside.

In the large bowl of an electric mixer cream the butter, add the two sugars and the molasses, and beat for several minutes on high speed. Dissolve the dry mustard in the vinegar and add to the molasses mixture. Beat in well. Add the egg, beat for 1 minute, and fold in the sifted flour mixture on low speed.

Form the dough into a 12-inch strip on a large sheet of waxed paper. Using the waxed paper to help, lift and roll the strip into a 12-inch cylinder. Wrap the cylinder in the waxed paper, twisting the ends of the paper to secure. Chill for two hours.

Preheat oven to 400 degrees.

Cut the roll into ¼-inch slices and arrange one inch apart on unbuttered cookie sheets. Bake for 10 to 12 minutes or until golden. Turn the cookie sheets around halfway through the baking time to insure even baking. Remove from the oven and allow the cookies to rest for 2 minutes before transferring to a cooling rack. Store in a tin.

Makes approximately 4 dozen large cookies.

• Spike a nut-bread recipe with a teaspoonful of dry mustard for extra nuttiness.

• Gingersnaps are snappier when a teaspoonful of dry mustard intensifies your favorite recipe.

3 ounces unsweetened
  chocolate
1¼ cups all-purpose flour
1 teaspoon baking powder
½ teaspoon cinnamon
½ cup butter, at room
  temperature

⅔ cup plus ½ cup
  granulated sugar
1 egg, at room temperature
1½ teaspoons dry mustard
2 tablespoons heavy cream

Melt the chocolate in a small heavy saucepan over low heat and set aside.

Sift together the flour, baking powder, and cinnamon, and set aside.

In the large bowl of an electric mixer cream together the butter and ⅔ cup of sugar. Add the melted chocolate and the egg and beat well. Dissolve the dry mustard in the heavy cream and add to the chocolate mixture. On the lowest speed, fold in the sifted flour mixture.

Divide the dough in half. Place each half on a sheet of waxed paper and form into a 10-inch strip. Using the waxed paper to help, lift and roll each strip into a 10-inch cylinder. Wrap each cylinder in the waxed paper, twisting the ends to secure. Chill for two hours.

Preheat oven to 375 degrees.

Cut the rolls into ¼-inch slices. Bake about one inch apart on unbuttered cookie sheets for about 10 minutes. Turn the cookie sheets around halfway through the baking time to insure even baking. Remove from the oven and allow the cookies to rest for 1 minute before transferring to a cooling rack.

Have the remaining ½ cup of sugar ready on a sheet of waxed paper. While the cookies are still warm, gently press into the sugar to coat both sides. Transfer to a cookie tin for storage.

Makes approximately 7 dozen small cookies.

• Spicy Zucchini Bread •

2 cups raw zucchini,
  unpeeled, coarsely grated
3 eggs, at room temperature
2 cups sugar
1 cup vegetable oil
3 cups all-purpose flour
2 teaspoons baking soda
1 teaspoon salt
¼ teaspoon baking powder
2 teaspoons dry mustard
½ teaspoon ginger
½ teaspoon cloves
1 tablespoon cinnamon
1 cup pecans, coarsely
  chopped

Preheat oven to 350 degrees.

Wash and dry the zucchini thoroughly. Grate on a four-sided hand grater, using coarse side, or in a processor, using shredding disk. Set aside in a colander to drain.

In a large bowl, using either a hand or electric mixer, beat the eggs until frothy, add the sugar gradually, and continue to beat on high speed for about 5 minutes, until the mixture is thick. Beat in the oil and zucchini on medium speed and mix well.

Sift together the flour, baking soda, salt, baking powder, mustard, ginger, cloves, and cinnamon, and stir into the zucchini mixture on low speed until thoroughly combined. With a rubber spatula fold in the nuts and pour batter into two 9 × 5 × 3-inch well-buttered loaf pans.

Bake for one hour. Let the loaves cool for 5 minutes. Invert onto a plate and remove pans. Invert again onto a cooling rack and cool right-side up. The loaves will keep, frozen, for up to 2 months.

Makes 2 loaves.

• After rolling out the dough for your favorite Schnecken recipe, sprinkle generously with brown sugar and equal amounts of cinnamon and dry mustard, then with raisins and crushed pecans. All the flavors will be accented by the mustard.

• Carrot Cake •

2 cups all-purpose flour
1 teaspoon baking soda
1 teaspoon baking powder
½ teaspoon salt
1 tablespoon dry mustard
2 teaspoons cinnamon
½ teaspoon ginger

2 cups sugar
1½ cups vegetable oil
4 eggs, at room temperature
3 cups raw carrots, finely
  grated
Optional: confectioners
  sugar

Preheat oven to 350 degrees.

Sift together the flour, baking soda, baking powder, salt, mustard, cinnamon, and ginger, and set aside.

Place the sugar and oil in the large bowl of an electric mixer. Beat together on high speed for 2 or 3 minutes until well combined. Turn to low speed and alternately add the sifted flour mixture and each of the eggs, beating until smooth after each addition. Fold in the grated carrots, then beat well for an additional minute on medium-high speed.

Pour the mixture into a well oiled 9-inch tube or Bundt pan. Bake for 1 hour and 20 minutes. Let the cake cool in the pan in an upright position. When cooled, invert onto a rack and lift off pan. Sprinkle with confectioners sugar, if desired.

• Add the zip of dry mustard to any cheese-bread batter to give the fragrant loaf a spicier, more memorable flavor.

• Be inventive with dry mustard: sprinkle a little (the first time try about ½ teaspoon) along with grated fresh ginger over a peach pie before baking to give an oriental touch to a favorite American sweet.

• Apple pie recipes get a boost in flavor by adding dry mustard to the cinnamon and sugar you sprinkle over the fruit.

• Fresh Ginger Gingerbread •

2½ cups all-purpose flour
1½ teaspoons baking soda
½ teaspoon baking powder
1 teaspoon cinnamon
½ teaspoon cloves
2 teaspoons dry mustard
½ cup butter, at room temperature

½ cup sugar
1 egg, at room temperature
1 cup unsulfured molasses
½ cup finely grated fresh ginger root
1 cup hot water

Preheat oven to 350 degrees.

Sift together the flour, baking soda, baking powder, cinnamon, cloves, and mustard. Set aside.

In the large bowl of an electric mixer cream together the butter and sugar until fluffy. Beat in the egg and molasses on medium speed for 1 minute. Add the fresh ginger and beat in thoroughly. On low speed add the flour mixture alternately with the hot water, beating after each addition. When everything is added, beat on high speed for 30 seconds, until smooth.

Pour the batter into a well buttered 9 × 9 × 2-inch pan. Bake for 45 to 50 minutes. Cool for 10 minutes. Turn out onto a cooling rack to cool completely or serve warm with sweetened whipped cream.

• Mustard Crepe Batter •

2 cups all-purpose flour
½ teaspoon salt
4 eggs
1 cup cold water
1 cup milk

4 tablespoons butter, melted, plus melted butter for skillet
3 tablespoons Dijon mustard

Sift together the flour and salt. Place all the ingredients in the container of a blender or processor fitted with steel blade. Process for 1 minute. Scrape down the sides with a rubber spatula and process 30 seconds longer. Place the batter in a covered jar or container and refrigerate for 2 hours or more.

Use a 6-inch crepe pan or skillet with sloping sides. Brush lightly with melted butter for the first crepe only. The first crepe may stick, but by the second crepe, the pan will be seasoned. Heat the pan over medium-high heat. Have the batter ready in a wide-mouthed pitcher (a 4-cup measuring container is ideal). Pour about 3 tablespoons of the batter into the hot pan, tilting the pan to coat the bottom surface completely. Quickly pour the excess back into the pitcher. You will soon get the rhythm of it and judge the proper amount of batter to pour each time. Set the skillet back on the heat and cook until the surface of the crepe becomes dull and loses all its gloss. Cook a few seconds longer, until the edges of the crepe begin to pull away from the pan. Have a large clean towel spread out on work surface. Invert the pan and bang the edge sharply to release the crepe upside down onto the surface of the towel. Repeat the process until all the batter is used. As the crepes cool, they may be stacked. There will be a "lip" on each crepe where the batter was poured off. This may be trimmed off later or left on and tucked in when crepes are rolled around a filling. The crepes are so thin that is unnecessary to cook both sides.

To fill, lay the crepe browned side up. Fill and roll so that the pale, uncooked side is facing out. Finish the crepes according to your recipe.

Fill the crepes with any savory filling such as creamed seafood or chicken, or vegetables such as spinach and mushrooms. Or brush each crepe with a thin layer of sour cream; top with thin slices of smoked salmon and fresh sprigs of dill. The crepes are also ideal for turning leftovers into elegant main courses.

Makes approximately two dozen 6-inch crepes.

Storing the crepes.: If the crepes are not to be filled immediately, store stacked, with two sheets of waxed paper in between each crepe. Place the stack on an aluminum foil dish and cover well with aluminum foil or plastic. They may be stored this way in the refrigerator for several days, or in the freezer for up to two months. The double layer of waxed paper enables you to remove any amount needed without damaging the rest. *Important:* do not attempt to fill and roll the crepes until they have reached room temperature, or they will crack.

• Mustard Beer Bread •

---

2 packages active dry yeast	1 cup Dijon mustard
½ cup lukewarm water	¼ cup plus 2 teaspoons
1 tablespoon sugar	white mustard seeds
½ cup butter	6 cups all-purpose flour
1 cup beer	1 egg white beaten with 1
2 teaspoons salt	tablespoon cold water

Dissolve the yeast in the lukewarm water, add the sugar, and set aside.

Melt the butter in a saucepan and stir in the beer, salt, mustard, and ¼ cup mustard seeds. Place this mixture in the bowl of an electric mixer fitted with a dough hook. Add the yeast mixture. On low speed add the flour 1 cup at a time and mix until the dough clings to the hook and leaves the sides of the bowl. Continue to knead on low speed for about 10 minutes, until the dough is smooth and elastic.

To mix by hand place the butter mixture and the yeast mixture in a large bowl. Add the flour 1 cup at a time and mix with a wooden spoon until a dough is formed. Turn out onto a lightly floured surface and knead for about 10 minutes, until the dough is smooth and elastic.

Place the dough in a warm, oiled bowl and oil the top of the dough. Vegetable oil is suitable. Cover the bowl with a clean dry towel and place in a warm spot (80 to 85 degrees), free from drafts. Allow to rise for two hours, until doubled in bulk. Punch down, cover again, and allow to rise for an additional hour. Divide the dough in half with a sharp knife and place in two well-greased loaf pans, 8½ × 4½ × 2½-inches. Cover and allow to rise for one-half hour in the pans before baking.

Preheat oven to 375 degrees.

With a sharp knife make three diagonal cuts on top of each loaf, about ½-inch deep. Brush the tops with the beaten egg white and water and lightly press a teaspoon of mustard seeds into top of each loaf of bread. Place a large baking pan of hot water on the floor of the oven. Bake the loaves for about 50 minutes or until they sound hollow when tapped. Brush the tops with cold water 3 or 4 times during the baking for a very crusty bread. Remove from the baking pans immediately when done, to prevent sogginess. Transfer to cooling racks and allow to cool completely, right side up.

Makes 2 loaves.

• If you like mincemeat pie, you'll like it even more with the tingle of a teaspoonful or two of dry mustard in the filling mixture.

• Plum puddings, fruit cakes, and pumpkin pies have more zest when a teaspoon of dry mustard is one of the ingredients.

• That traditional Viennese confection, Linzer Torte, becomes untraditional and international in flavor when a teaspoon of dry mustard is combined with the other spices and cocoa in the dough.

• Fill baked apples with Mostarda di Frutta—Italian preserved fruits in mustard oil—sprinkle with cream sherry, and bake as usual. Unusually piquant.

• Try using Mustard Butter in your favorite puff paste recipe when making pastry shells for *vol-au-vent,* or in any savory filling.

BASICS

• Short-Pastry Dough •

2 cups all-purpose flour
½ teaspoon salt
½ cup butter, cold

4 tablespoons vegetable
  shortening, cold
4 to 5 tablespoons ice water

Place the flour and salt in a bowl. Make a well in the center. Cut the butter and shortening into small pieces and place in the well. Using either a pastry blender or your fingers, work rapidly and blend the butter and shortening into the flour until the mixture is like coarse meal. Sprinkle the water on the mixture and work in by hand until a dough forms. The dough should be handled as little as possible to prevent it from becoming tough. Do not use more water unless it is necessary. Gather the dough together until it forms a ball and leaves the sides of the bowl cleanly. If you are making a 2-crust pie, split the dough in half and shape into 2 flattened balls. Wrap each in waxed paper and refrigerate for 30 minutes before rolling out. It's a good idea, even if you need only half the recipe, to make both crusts, roll them out, form 2 pie shells, and freeze one for future use.

To make the pastry dough in a food processor, fit the container with the steel blade. Place the flour and salt in the container, add the pieces of butter and shortening, and use several on-off motions to obtain the texture of coarsely ground meal. Add the water and run the motor for 1 minute until the dough is formed. Scrape down the sides of the container with a rubber spatula and process for 30 seconds longer. The dough will leave the sides of the container. Proceed to shape into flattened balls and wrap in waxed paper as above.

To roll out, remove the dough from the refrigerator. If it seems very hard, allow the dough to rest for about 5 minutes. On a lightly floured surface, using a floured rolling pin, roll out the flattened ball, working from the center out and turning the dough to shape an even circle. Roll it out to ⅛-inch thick, large enough to overlap the pie pan. An easy way to fit the dough into the pan is to fold the finished circle, first in half, then in half again. Lift it and place the point in the center of the pie pan. Unfold the dough and it will be centered. Press the dough lightly into the pan and trim the edge for a 1-crust pie. Pinch all around the edge with your fingertips to form a pattern or press with a fork. For a 2-crust pie trim the edge, leaving a slight overhang. Roll out the second circle in the same manner as the first, place over the filled bottom crust, and turn the overhang back over the top crust. Press the edges together to seal and trim neatly. Using your fingertips pleat the edges together or press with a fork. Bake according to the recipe.

Makes pastry for a 2-crust 9-inch pie.

• Chicken Stock •

---

3 pounds chicken necks, wings, and backs
3 quarts cold water
2 celery stalks, including leafy top, cut crosswise in 2
2 carrots, scraped, cut crosswise in 2
1 large onion stuck with 2 cloves

Several sprigs of fresh parsley
6 peppercorns
1 large clove garlic, peeled
Salt to taste
1 teaspoon dried rosemary leaves
1 large bay leaf, split in half

Place all the ingredients in a large pot. Bring to a boil over high heat and skim off any accumulated scum on the

---

surface. Reduce the heat to medium, cover, and simmer for 2 hours.

Remove the pot from the heat, strain the stock, and discard the solids. Pour the stock into pint- or quart-sized containers. When cooled place in refrigerator or freezer. The fat will rise to the surface when chilled and is then easy to remove. For smaller quantities, to keep on hand freeze the stock in ice cube trays, remove the frozen cubes, and store in plastic bags. The stock will keep, refrigerated, for 1 week, and up to 2 months in the freezer. Reheat before using.

Makes approximately 3 quarts.

• Beef Stock •

4 pounds meaty beef bones (short ribs, shin bones)	1 leek, trimmed, split down center
4 quarts cold water	Several sprigs of fresh parsley
2 celery stalks, including leafy top, cut crosswise in 2	6 peppercorns
	3 cloves garlic, peeled
2 carrots, scraped, cut crosswise in 2	Salt to taste
	1 teaspoon dried thyme leaves
1 large onion stuck with 2 cloves	1 large bay leaf, split in half

Place all the ingredients in a large pot. Bring to a boil over high heat and skim off any accumulated scum rising to the surface. Reduce the heat to medium, cover, and simmer for 4 hours.

Remove the pot from the heat; strain and discard the solids, except for the meat, which makes an excellent meal when served with Herb Sauce (page 190) or horseradish and mustard. Store the strained stock as suggested in the preceding recipe.

Makes approximately 4 quarts.

• Mustard Dumplings •

2 cups all-purpose flour	4 tablespoons butter
4 teaspoons baking powder	¼ cup chopped fresh
1 teaspoon salt	parsley
½ teaspoon white pepper	⅔ cup milk
4 teaspoons dry mustard	2 eggs, slightly beaten

In a small bowl sift together the flour, baking powder, salt, pepper, and dry mustard. Cut in the butter with a pastry blender or your fingers until the mixture resembles coarse meal. Toss in the parsley, add the milk and eggs, and mix with a wooden spoon, stirring briefly just to absorb the flour.

Cook the dumplings by adding to any simmering stew. Drop by tablespoonsful into the gravy, cover, and steam them for 15 to 20 minutes, until puffed and dry. They may also be cooked in broth or water by adding them a few at a time to the simmering liquid, covering, and cooking for 15 to 20 minutes. Remove with a slotted spoon. Use an ample amount of liquid, as dumplings swell with cooking.

Add to chicken or beef stews 20 minutes or so before end of cooking time.

Makes approximately 12 large dumplings.

• Clarified Butter •

To clarify butter place the butter in a small heavy saucepan and melt slowly over low heat. When completely melted, pour off the clear liquid and reserve, discarding the milky residue at the bottom. Clarified butter can be made in large quantities and stored in the refrigerator for later use.

AFTERWORD

Now that you've cooked with mustard, there are a few other uses for it around the house.

- After peeling and chopping onions or garlic, rub powdered mustard into your hands and rinse in warm water to remove the odor.

- Add a heaping tablespoon of dry mustard to the dishwasher along with the soap to remove odors, especially those of fish and onions, from dishes, pots, and plastic utensils.

- A few teaspoonsful of dry mustard in a bucket of mussels or clams make the mollusks gasp out bits of grit and sand.

And you can decorate with mustard and mustard paraphernalia.

- To make a pretty mustard spreader, trim the root end of a stalk of scallion, cut the green top down to about four inches long, and make crisscross cuts about one inch deep in the green end to create a fringe. Cover with ice water and chill for two hours to curl fringe. Stick fringed end into mustard pot; wield like a paint brush.

- If you don't own a decorative mustard pot, create your own. Cut a thin slice from the stem end of a fresh lemon (to make a solid base), then cut off one-third of the lemon from the other end and reserve it. Scoop out the pulp, leaving the skin and pith intact, and fill with mustard. Cut a notch into the edge of the reserved third to accomodate the neck of a small spoon and use as a cover. Try it, too, with a red or green bell pepper.

• Collect mustard pots to fill with your own homemade mustards. Set out a selection to have with a country pâté, cold meatloaf, or a fish terrine.

SOURCES
FOR
IMPORTED
MUSTARDS

Although Dijon mustards are distributed everywhere in the U.S. and Canada, sold in department stores, food-specialty shops, gourmet shops, neighborhood mom-and-pop stores, and most supermarkets, you may still have trouble locating a fresh supply in your area. The following is a regional listing of mustard importers. They do not sell to consumers directly; however, they can give you the names of retailers nearby if you call or write to them.

New England

Bond Foods, Inc.
11 Crary St., Providence, RI 02903 (401) 421-4136

Chex Finer Foods, Inc.
39 F.R. McKay Drive, Attleboro, MA 02703
(617) 226-0660

Crabtree & Evelyn Ltd.
P.O. Box 167, Woodstock, CT 06281 (203) 928-2766

Crystal Food Import Corp.
245 Sumner St., East Boston, MA 02128 (617) 569-7500

France America
6 Stoddard Rd., Hingham, MA 02043 (617) 749-0426

S.E. Rykoff
221 N. Beacon St., Boston, MA 02135 (617) 254-0300
8 Commercial St., Concord, NH 03301 (603) 224-3372

A & A Food Products/Richter Brothers
801 Washington Ave., Carlstadt, NJ 07072
(201) 935-6850 & (800) 526-6282

Amazone Tea & Coffee
35-17 31st St., Long Island City, NY 11106
(212) 726-3100

American Roland Foods
46 W. 24th St., New York, NY 10010 (212) 741-8799

Arbee Fine Foods
250 W. Nyack Rd., West Nyack, NY 10994
(212) 567-0800

Arthur Schuman, Inc.
P.O. Box 2039, 1029 Teaneck Rd., Teaneck, NJ 07666
(201) 837-4090

Bonvego 16 Ltd.
19 Kensington Rd., Bronxville, NY 10708 (914) 337-2206

Broad Hollow Farm Products
340 Broad Hollow Rd., East Farmingdale, NY 11735
(516) 249-2222

Captain Post Co.
556 W. 52nd St., New York, NY 10019 (212) 586-5773

Classique Foods (div. M.H. Greenbaum)
165 Chambers St., New York, NY 10007 (212) 349-4300

Commerce Foods (div. Roth & Liebman)
401 Broadway, New York, NY 10013 (212) 925-2020

Embassy Grocery Corp.
57-10 49th St., Maspeth, NY 11378 (212) 366-8200

Europa Foods
1 Lexington Ave., Bethpage, NY 11714 (516) 822-5336

Haddon House Food Products
P.O. Box 398, Marlton Pike, Medford, NJ 08055
(215) 923-0536

Haram Christensen Corp.
34 Ericsson Pl., New York, NY 10013 (212) 925-4883

International Marketing Services
415 Lexington Ave., Suite 700, New York, NY 10022
(212) 599-2929

T.G. Koryn (div. Lankor Inter.)
66 Broad St., Carlstadt, NJ 07072 (201) 935-4500

Melba Food Specialties
186 Huron St., Brooklyn, NY 11222 (212) 383-3142

New York Food Specialties
420 Bergen Blvd., Palisades Park, NJ 07650
(201) 944-0821

Reese Finer Foods
519 W. 16th St., New York, NY 10011, (212) 924-3011

Robin Packing Company Inc.
179 Duane St., New York, NY 10013 (212) 925-3321

A. Sargenti Co.
453 W. 17th St., New York, NY 10011 (212) 989-8888

Sunshine Wholesale Grocery
2245 Broadway, New York, NY 10024 (212) 787-3810

Middle Atlantic

Castle Food Products
2730 Lock Raven Rd., Baltimore, MD 21218
(301) 889-8400

Dairy King, Inc.
703 Nursery Rd., Linthicum Heights, MD 21090
(701) 636-1400

Diamond Food Products
766-68 9th St., Philadelphia, PA 19147 (215) 925-1230

Donnerex International Inc.
Wynnewood Center, Suite 216, 50 E. Wynnewood Rd.,
Wynnewood, PA 19096 (215) 896-5181

Fancy Foods of Virginia
731-743 E. 25th St., Norfolk, VA 23504 (804) 627-9568

Gourm-e-co Imports
1200 First St., Alexandria, VA 22314 (703) 548-4204

International Food Distributors
1340 Crease St., Philadelphia, PA 19125 (415) 423-3775

The George B. Travis Associates
3408 Wisconsin Ave. NW, Washington, DC 20016
(202) 363-9695

Trymor Food Co.
3020 Darnell Rd., Philadelphia, PA 19154 (215) 632-3131

South East

Atlanta Wholesale Foods
789 Miami Circle, Atlanta, GA 30324 (404) 266-1317

Edward Kelly & Sons
2260 NW 13th Ave., Miami, FL 33142 (305) 634-2684

Lieber Foods Inc.
244 Peter St. SW, Atlanta, GA 30313 (404) 688-1600

Market Food Distributors
4598 E. 10th La., Miami, FL 33012 (305) 688-6572

Mutual Wholesale
4100 N. 29th Terrace, Hollywood, FL 33020
(305) 927-0543

Quality Sweets Inc.
2975 44th St. N., St. Petersburg, FL 33714 (813) 525-4716

Reese Finer Foods
1320 White St. SW, Atlanta, GA 30310 (404) 758-9111

Southern Season
Eastgate, Chapel Hill, NC 37514 (919) 929-7133

Specialty Food Distributors
8408 East Tample Terrace Hwy., Tampa, FL 33617
(813) 988-9123

Swiss Chalet Fine Foods
5501 NW 79 Ave., Miami, FL 33166 (305) 592-0008

Tri-State Wholesale Inc.
2490 Halls Mill Rd., Mobile, AL 36606 (205) 473-4765

Great Lakes

Berto Fancy Foods Inc.
7416 N. Milwaukee Ave., Niles, IL 60648 (312) 647-9747

Charlotte Charles Inc.
2501 North Elston Ave., Chicago, IL 60647
(312) 772-8310

Dae-Julie
4500 West Dickens Ave., Chicago, IL 60639
(312) 342-9100

Kramer Food Company
32021 Edwards Rd., Madison Heights, MI 48071
(313) 585-8141

Lyndale Finer Foods
5101 Creek Rd., Cincinnati, OH 45242 (513) 791-3025

Reese Finer Foods
1100 Kirk St., Elk Grove Village, IL 60007 (312) 595-7900

Symon's General Store
401 East Lake St., Petoskey, MI 49770 (616) 347-2438

Towner Associates
1924 Packard Rd., Ann Arbor, MI 48104 (313) 769-0865

North Central

J.A. Demonchaux
827 N. Kansas Ave., Topeka, KS 66608 (913) 235-1588

Gourmet Foods Inc.
860 Vandalia, St. Paul, MN 55114 (612) 646-2981

Louis Albert & Son Foods Co. Inc.
P.O. Box 55, Ames Ave. Station, Omaha, NE 68111
(402) 451-9312

Swiss American Importing Co.
4354 Clayton Avenue, St. Louis, MO 63110
(314) 533-2224

Antone's Import Co.
805-901 Rhode Pl., Houston, TX 77019 (713) 526-1046

Fancifood (div. of Universal Foods Inc.)
1201 Oliver St., Houston, TX 77007 (713) 861-6467

Gerde Institutional Food Service Co.
P.O. Box 61028, New Orleans, LA 70161 (504) 733-5200

Gourmet France
2452 Walnut Ridge St., Dallas, TX 75229 (214) 241-8164

Reese Finer Foods
5709 Armour Dr., Houston, TX 77020 (713) 672-9339

Wines Unlimited
3847 Baronne St., New Orleans, LA 70115
(504) 897-0191

Mountain

Denver Gourmet Foods Distributors
3870 D. Niagara, Denver, CO 80207 (303) 355-9233

Fancifood (div. of Universal Foods Inc.)
3929 S. 500 West, Salt Lake City, UT 84107
(801) 266-8167

Glenn Bowlus Distributing Co.
P.O. Box 11390, Phoenix, AZ 85061 (602) 269-8902

Idaho Food Products Inc.
P.O. Box 1638, 1721 Main St., Boise, ID 83701
(208) 343-7507

Needlers Imports
1501 South Pearl St., Denver, CO 80210 (303) 733-8606

Reese Finer Foods
1617 W. 12 Ave., Denver, CO 80204 (303) 623-2742

S.E. Rykoff & Co.
1637 E. 18th Street, Tucson, AZ 85719 (602) 623-4709
2101 Stephens, Missoula, MT 59801 (406) 728-4590
5115 S. Industrial Rd., Las Vegas, NV 89118
(702) 739-7075

Southwestern Grocery Inc.
177 Toole Ave., P.O. Box 12985, Tucson, AZ 85732
(602) 623-7541

Pacific

Crozier Food Products Corp.
24335 Narbonne Ave., Lomita, CA 90717 (213) 325-0388
938 N. 200th St., Seattle, WA 98133 (206) 546-5178
95/181 Waikalani Dr., Wahawa, HI 96786 (808) 623-3600

DeVries Import
1811 Pontius Ave., Los Angeles, CA 90025
(213) 473-5226

Eurobest Foods Corp.
8114 SW Nimbus Ave., Beaverton, OR 97005
(503) 643-7426

Ever Fresh Foods Corp.
4200 S. Alemeda, Los Angeles, CA 90058 (213) 231-9346

Fancifood, (div. of Universal Foods Inc.)
343 Oyster Point Blvd., San Francisco, CA 94080
(415) 871-7180

Floyd Peterson Co.
3231 20th Ave. W., Seattle, WA 98199 (206) 282-4215

Gourmet France
9373 Remick Ave., Pacoima, CA 91331 (213) 768-4300
3095 Kerner Blvd., San Rafael, CA 94901 (415) 456-2900

Gourmet Specialties
2250 McKinnon Ave., San Francisco, CA 94124
(415) 648-7300

Information & Merchandising Service Inc.
184 Cobblestone Dr., San Rafael, CA 94903 (415)
472-2252

Jacob Hamburger Co., Inc.
5300 N. Channel Ave., Swan Island, P.O. Box 4468,
  Portland, OR 97208 (503) 285-4531

Madiera Sales Co.
45 S. Linden Ave., South San Francisco, CA 94080
(415) 873-1204

A. Magnano & Sons
1502 4th Ave. S., Seattle, WA 98134 (206) 622-3021

The Napoleon Co.
1510 Norton Bldg., Seattle, WA 98104 (206) 622-0720

Reese Finer Foods
5416 Union Pacific Ave., City of Commerce, CA 90022
(213) 726-0900

S.E. Rykoff & Co.
1429 130th Ave. NE, Bellevue, WA 98005
(206) 455-1911

S & K. Sales Co.
97-731 Kam Hwy., Pearl City, HI 96782 (808) 455-4164

Scondia Finer Foods
1132 Beecher St., San Leandro, CA 94577 (415) 632-1742

Sonoma Mission Foods
P.O. Box 2344, South San Francisco, CA 94080
(415) 761-4790

Young's Market Company
500 S. Central Ave., Los Angeles, CA 90013
(213) 629-5571

Puerto Rico

Plaza Provisions
G.P.O. Box 3328, San Juan, PR 00936 (809) 767-7070

INDEX